PRAISE FOR REDUCING

The search for the holy grail of investing has intensified since 2014 with development of new investor alternatives facilitating more efficient strategies for investors. Swedroe and Grogan clearly present and illustrate this path to improved investment performance to the benefit of us all.

— JOHN A. HASLEM, PROFESSOR EMERITUS OF FINANCE,
ROBERT H. SMITH SCHOOL OF BUSINESS, UNIVERSITY OF MARYLAND

New to this edition is a practical guide to finding alternative investments to black-swan proof your portfolio. Swedroe's books on investment mistakes, factor investing and now this one form the backbone of my investment strategies course. My students love the way his books help them think clearly, write crisply, and guide them to new discoveries.

— ED TOWER, PROFESSOR OF ECONOMICS, DUKE UNIVERSITY

Reducing the Risk of Black Swans does an excellent job describing a set of unique alternative investments, which can be used to build portfolios with less downside risk without sacrificing expected returns. Investment pros should read this book.

— WESLEY R. GRAY, PH.D., CEO OF ALPHA ARCHITECT
AND CO-AUTHOR OF *QUANTITATIVE MOMENTUM*

THE RISK OF BLACK SWANS

Jumping out of airplane offers a much more thrilling experience than riding a bicycle down the street. But what if skydiving were as safe as riding that bike? Swedroe and Grogan pose the financial equivalent to that question in their updated book, *Reducing the Risk of Black Swans: Using the Science of Investing to Capture Returns with Less Volatility.* This new edition introduces some newly available products. By coupling such products with Nobel Prize winning theory, Swedroe and Grogan explain how investors can earn higher rewards, while taking lower levels of risk.

— ANDREW HALLAM, AUTHOR OF *MILLIONAIRE TEACHER: THE NINE RULES OF WEALTH YOU SHOULD HAVE LEARNED IN SCHOOL* AND *MILLIONAIRE EXPAT: HOW TO BUILD WEALTH LIVING OVERSEAS*

If the holy grail of investing is many dependable but uncorrelated sources of return, then Swedroe and Grogan have charted a valuable course for investors. This book covers a variety of traditional and alternative risk premia and anomalies, supported by a tsunami of evidence, and rounded out with fund and ETF recommendations. Market conditions may offer auspicious timing for this book, but the takeaways are timeless. Get it and read it for better investment outcomes.

— ADAM BUTLER, CHIEF INVESTMENT OFFICER, RESOLVE ASSET MANAGEMENT

REDUCING THE RISK OF

BLACK SWANS

REDUCING THE RISK OF

BLACK SWANS

USING THE SCIENCE OF INVESTING TO
CAPTURE RETURNS WITH LESS VOLATILITY

LARRY SWEDROE & KEVIN GROGAN

FOREWORD BY ROSS STEVENS

2018 EDITION

BAM ALLIANCE Press
8182 Maryland Ave
Suite 500
St. Louis, MO 63105
thebamalliance.com

Design by Alan Dubinsky
Layout by Alan Dubinsky & Dave Vander Maas

CONTENTS

ACKNOWLEDGEMENTS

For all their support and encouragement, we thank our colleagues at Buckingham Strategic Wealth and The BAM ALLIANCE, with special thanks to Dan Campbell for his help with the data. In addition, we would like to thank the research staffs at AQR Capital Management (specifically Anti Ilmanen, Ronen Israel and Toby Moskowitz, as well as Mark McClennan), Bridgeway Capital Management (especially Andrew Berkin), and Dimensional Fund Advisors (especially Jim Davis, Marlena Lee and Weston Wellington, as well as Bo Cornell).

We would also like to acknowledge the contributions of Adam Butler, Wes Gray, John Haslem and Ed Tower, each of whom reviewed the book and offered valuable suggestions.

Larry thanks his wife, Mona, the love of his life, for her tremendous encouragement and understanding during the lost weekends and many nights he sat at the computer well into the early morning hours. She has always provided whatever support was needed — and then some. Walking through life with her has truly been a gracious experience.

Kevin thanks his wife, Julie, who makes every day a joy, for her love and patience. He also thanks his parents, brother and sister-in-law, who have always supported him and had his best interests in mind.

Finally, we express our great appreciation to Ross Stevens of Stone Ridge for providing the foreword.

The usual caveat applies that any remaining mistakes are ours.

PREFACE

The first edition of this book was published in 2014. In that version, we showed how investors could create more efficient portfolios using what we refer to as the science of investing. Such portfolios, built on evidence from peer-reviewed academic journals, not only have delivered higher risk-adjusted returns, but also have significantly reduced the negative impact of rare, downside events, known as "black swans."

Since 2014, favorable developments have led us to conclude that the time to update the book had arrived. The most important development has been the "retailization" of investment strategies once solely the domain of hedge funds and institutional investors. The good news is that mutual fund sponsors have been bringing these strategies to the public in the form of vehicles regulated under the Investment Act of 1940, with expense ratios well below those of the traditional 2 percent of assets and 20 percent of profits, or "2/20," fee structure of hedge funds.

Because many hedge fund strategies involve investing in illiquid investments (allowing investors to access the illiquidity premium), fund sponsors had to develop an alternative to the open-end mutual fund structure that provides daily liquidity. An example of a strategy that requires an alternative structure is investing in longer-term consumer loans, such as a student loan. You cannot make a three-, five- or seven-year loan if the capital you need to originate it can be withdrawn on a daily basis. Another example is investing in reinsurance contracts, which typically are for one year. The interval fund structure was developed to address this issue.

An interval fund is a closed-end investment company that periodically (typically quarterly) offers to buy back a stated portion of its shares from shareholders. However, while interval funds are valued daily, their shares typically do not trade on the secondary market like other closed-end funds.

Another important development has been the "fintech revolution." Firms such as Lending Club, Square and SoFi have been utilizing technology to disintermediate traditional lenders, such as banks, in the consumer, small business and student loan lending markets. Their lower costs have enabled them to offer more attractive rates than traditional banks. These firms need committed sources of longer-term capital to make term loans and provide immediate funding to borrowers. Interval funds partner with such lenders, providing investors access to these markets.

These developments have enabled retail investors to access new and unique sources of risk and returns. Each of the alternative investments we will discuss have equity-like forward-looking return expectations that show low to no correlation to the returns of the traditional stocks and bonds dominant in portfolios. The combination of equity-like returns and low correlation allows investors to build more efficient portfolios than when the first edition of this book was published.

It is important to understand that none of the five alternatives we will discuss are new investments. As previously mentioned, in many cases they have resided for decades on the balance sheets of hedge funds and endowments. Now that they are available to financial advisors and investors without the higher fees typically associated with hedge funds, we are including them in our client portfolios.

Part I of this book updates the data from the original work. Part II offers our insights on five alternative investments that can add greater efficiency to your portfolio and further reduce the negative impact of the dreaded black swan.

FOREWORD

Most individual investors' portfolios are dominated by two asset classes: public domestic equities and bonds, the "risky" and "safe" asset classes, respectively. This traditional portfolio (colloquially referred to as "60/40," reflecting an allocation of 60 percent equities and 40 percent bonds) has performed extremely well over the last 30 years and enabled millions of investors to meet their objectives of purchasing a home, paying for college, and ultimately funding a more secure retirement. However, this performance has been driven by a number of favorable tailwinds — a secular decline in interest rates, favorable demographics, globalization, financial deregulation and the "democratization of investing" — many of which are unlikely to have the same impact going forward. This creates an acute challenge for today's investors who may have the same goals as the prior generation, but will be unable to rely on the traditional portfolio to deliver the required returns.

A primary culprit is interest rates. Short-term interest rates across the developed world now hover around zero, with longer-dated bond yields at or near all-time lows. The days of putting money in a bank account and getting 5 percent or getting 8 percent in longer-duration bonds are gone, and unlikely to return any time soon. This is a critical issue because *all* asset classes price relative to cash. For example, if bank accounts yield 5 percent then equities might be priced to earn a return of 9 percent to induce investors to take equity risk; but if bank accounts yield 0 percent, investors are willing to hold equities even if they expect to earn far less, say 4 percent, because it still beats getting zero. In other words, low rates mean that *all* assets are now priced to earn lower returns.

While low interest rates themselves represent a drag on portfolio returns, they also create an asymmetric risk. There is likely limited room for rates to go much lower to boost returns, but a whole lot of room for them to go up, weighing returns down. The last time the United States experienced a long-term rise in interest rates from such lows began about 50 years ago, and it was a time period investors would soon rather forget. From 1964 through 1981, as rates were generally rising, the annualized excess returns (i.e., the returns an investor could get above what he could get by putting his money in a bank account) of the 60/40 portfolio were -1.4 percent *before taking out taxes and fees*.

And it's not just that anemic yields today are suppressing future expected returns. Low rates are also *increasing the risk* in fixed income allocations. With rates coming down so much, the duration[1] of bonds has increased (e.g., the duration of the Barclays Capital U.S. Aggregate Bond Index has gone from a low of 3.7 years at the beginning of 2009 to 6.0 years in January 2018 — health warning: This is *exactly* like levering your fixed income portfolio 62 percent during this time period; did you mean to do that?), which means that forthcoming increases in rates will have an even more pronounced impact on returns. It's a double whammy.

---

[1] Duration is a measure of the sensitivity of a bond's price to changes in interest rates, expressed as a number of years.

If we narrow the lens to a more recent time period, post the 2008-2009 financial crisis, it's likely that not all investors appreciate the historical uniqueness of the last eight years. Fueled by the combined sugar high of unprecedented central bank asset purchases, and the irresistible siren song of recency bias, the pain and memory of the financial crisis has been comfortably, if only temporarily and quite dangerously, numbed. Consider the following:

- Since March 2009, the 60/40 portfolio has delivered annualized excess returns of 12.7 percent, annualized volatility of 6.9 percent, and a Sharpe ratio of 1.8. The 90-year average for the 60/40 portfolio is 5.0 percent annualized excess returns, with 12.0 percent annualized volatility, and a Sharpe ratio of 0.4. So compared to the long-term average, post-crisis the 60/40 portfolio has enjoyed 2.5 times the annualized excess return, about 40 percent less volatility, and more than 4.5 times the Sharpe ratio.

- If we limit the analysis to stocks, as we begin 2018, we just experienced the only calendar year in which the S&P 500 Index had positive returns every month, with the streak now growing to 15 months. In addition, the S&P 500 Index has been profitable in 22 out of the last 23 months, which has never happened. And during this stretch, the Sharpe ratio of the S&P 500 has been 3.3, *10 times its historical average.* Is there a more crowded trade in capital markets today? Is there an asset class with a stronger sense of entitlement to positive, long-term returns among its owners? Let's remember first principles: A stock entitles its holder to the *last* claim on the cash flow of a company, after the firm pays rent, insurance, interest, compensation, cost of goods sold, etc. If, and only if, there's anything left over, the equity owner gets it. Instead, lately stocks have been acting like they are the *first* claim on the cash flows of a company. It's not supposed to be this easy to make so much money, especially with such remarkable consistency.

Going back to the 60/40 portfolio, try the following thought experiment: Holding volatility constant at the long-term average, what would annualized excess returns have to be over the next 10 and 20 years, for the post-crisis 60/40 portfolio Sharpe ratio to be equal to the long-term average?

The answer: Negative 2.6 percent annualized return for the next 10 years, and positive 1.2 percent annualized return for the next 20 years. Imagine making essentially no money on your investments for the next 10 or 20 years. No, really, stop and think about it for a moment. What would that mean for you?

Thankfully, enter Larry and Kevin!

As the dynamic duo explain in this extremely insightful and extraordinarily practical new book, one way to escape this dilemma is conceptually simple and entirely consistent with the tenets of modern portfolio theory: Add new return streams that can both a) provide returns consistent with what investors need going forward to *grow their wealth*, and b) provide sufficient diversification so that investors can *protect their wealth*.

Larry and Kevin show that instead of "turning the dial" *away from bonds* toward more of the same risky assets that are already in the portfolio (e.g., equities, high-yield credit, etc.), investors can now *turn it toward* investments that can maintain, or even enhance, the *future* return profile of their portfolios, but in a way that does not increase risk, and, in fact, almost surely decreases it.

What other types of investments offer potential returns consistent with those of riskier assets like equities, and can provide diversification properties that will allow investors to reduce risk? And if the solution is so obvious, why haven't investors embraced these new types of investments before?

There are two explanations which, taken together, are why this book makes such a significant contribution. First, many of these return streams haven't historically been accessible as investments. Second, investors suffer from an acute form of regret syndrome, i.e., don't do anything too different out of fear you might underperform relative to doing nothing at all. The first of these is changing fast; and with it, investors must change their mindset from one driven by fear of the unfamiliar. A major contribution of this book is reframing the "unfamiliar" as, in fact, quite familiar. The sources of some of the risk premiums Larry and Kevin discuss — particularly (re)insurance, lending and the VRP — have been around longer than stocks.

The reality is that we are standing at the front end of a long-term shift in how risk is held, but most investors don't know it yet. Quiet as this shift in risk-holding has been, though, it really is a revolution, not a fad. Here's how you can tell: When one party finds a way to make money by taking advantage of another, that's a fad — at some point, the disadvantaged party will learn to avoid the trap. When innovation creates a situation where everybody can be better off than they were, that's a revolution.

The first wave of revolutionary financial innovation "democratized investments" by making it possible for large numbers of investors to access the equity and bond markets via lower-cost mutual funds and ETFs. The second wave, now just underway, involves "democratizing balance sheets," uncovering a much broader array of risks arising from financial intermediation — by banks, (re)insurance companies and market-makers — and making them available in cost-efficient structures.

In this second wave, together we shift risk-holding from a tiny number of gigantic balance sheets to a gigantic number of tiny balance sheets. Together, we unlock profitable business lines historically buried within financial institutions. Together, we de-risk the financial system. And, together, we empower access to valuable P&L streams that can diversify the 60/40 portfolio.

However, to ride this second wave, I invite readers to be grateful that Larry and Kevin are their guides.

As Larry and Kevin explain, the investable universe is much, much larger than what most investors realize. For example, there are countless sources of returns that have been available *within* financial institutions, whose lending, trading and underwriting activity has generated a steady stream of profits over centuries. A wide range of these exposures once considered "un-investable," *or, more fundamentally, not even thought of as sources of returns,* are now increasingly available through new securities and funds.

Larry and Kevin guide the way with an engaging and actionable tour of alternative sources of risk premiums that are intuitive, pervasive and persistent — and their book is quite specific in exactly how, and how much, of this risk to take. Most importantly, they frame the landscape in the language of an investor: Will making changes to my portfolio increase my probability of being able to live the life I want, maybe even discover a life I didn't know was available, with the peace of mind that comes from knowing my tail risk is reduced?

Larry and Kevin show us that, starkly, investors now have a choice to make. Do they comfortably fail or uncomfortably succeed? Failing comfortably means investing largely as before; succeeding uncomfortably means adopting a new mindset and fundamentally altering what portfolios look like. Making this change implies turning the traditional portfolio inside-out, where core holdings become the satellites and a new breed of alternative risk premiums become the core. This is going to be a huge change, and many investors won't get there overnight. But the path forward has been illuminated, and the direction is clear.

Finally, a personal request: Before you read this book, please pause for a few minutes and take a quiet moment alone. Think about some of the things you have in your life that make you smile: family, friends, health, work. I find that a mental framework built around wanting what you already have is a better strategy for happiness than having what you want. Happiness is something we get to decide on in advance. After your pause, please then read the last appendix in this book, titled "Enough." It captures what this book is *really* about, and shares Larry and Kevin's deepest wisdom and most important messages. It's one of the best pieces of financial writing I've read anywhere, ever. "Enough" also captures why folks like Larry, Kevin and I — who devote their lives to helping others achieve peace of mind through financial security — run smiling to work in the morning. We get to do what we love.

Enjoy!

Ross L. Stevens
Founder, Stone Ridge
January 2018

INTRODUCTION

This book was written for those looking to expand their knowledge of the evidence-based investing world. In this world, evidence and peer-reviewed academic research, not instinct, opinion, or ego, are used to design portfolios. Whether you are an advisor looking to better serve your clients, an investor looking to become more knowledgeable about the workings of your portfolio, or even a financial oracle, you will benefit from this book. While it is short in length, its content is heavy. It is data-rich and full of detailed examples. The empty rhetoric or the distracting noise often heard in the active investment world has no place here. Science and hard data make our case. There is no need for elaborate prose or the hyperbolic statements so frequently heard on the other side of the investing aisle.

You are about to embark on a journey that we hope will be both informative and of great value. It is a roadmap to the holy grail of investing — an investment strategy that can deliver higher returns without increased risk, or the same return with reduced risk. Consider your search ended.

Finally, if you tend to be daunted by data or unfamiliar terms, don't worry. We have made great efforts to explain concepts in as simple terms as possible. Take your time, and know that by reading this book, you are taking steps toward becoming a better, more informed, hands-on investor. And that is something of which you can be proud.

PART I

USING THE SCIENCE OF INVESTING TO BUILD MORE EFFICIENT PORTFOLIOS

CHAPTER 1:
HOW TO THINK ABOUT
EXPECTED STOCK RETURNS

An important part of the process of developing an investment plan is estimating future returns to stocks and bonds. Unfortunately, many investors make two big mistakes when doing so. The first is to simply extrapolate past returns into the future. This is a mistake because it ignores the fact that current stock valuations play a very important role in determining future returns. Consider the following.

From 1926 through 1979, the S&P 500 Index returned 9.0 percent. From 1980 through 1999, it returned 17.9 percent, raising the return over the full period by 2.3 percentage points to 11.3 percent. Investors in 1999 using the historical return of 11.3 percent as a predictor of future returns were highly likely to be disappointed because they failed to take into account the fact that the earnings yield (the inverse of the price/earnings ratio) had fallen all the way from 11.4 percent to 3.5 percent. And lower earnings yields predict lower, not higher, future returns.

While the historical real return to stocks from 1926 through 2016 has been 6.9 percent (9.8 percent nominal return minus 2.9 percent inflation), most financial economists are now forecasting real returns well below that level. No metric for estimating future returns is generally agreed upon as the best, but the Shiller CAPE 10 (cyclically adjusted price-to-earnings) ratio is considered by many to be at least as good as, if not better than, others because it explains a significant portion (about 40 percent) of the variation in future returns. The CAPE 10 ratio uses smoothed real earnings over the prior 10 years to eliminate fluctuations in net income caused by variations in profit margins over a typical business cycle.

The first to argue for smoothing a firm's earnings over a longer term were value investors Benjamin Graham and David Dodd. In their classic text, *Security Analysis*, Graham and Dodd noted one-year earnings were too volatile to offer a good idea of a firm's true earning power. Decades later, Yale economist and Nobel Prize winner Robert Shiller popularized the 10-year version of Graham and Dodd's price-to-earnings (P/E) measure as a way to value the stock market.

In an attempt to minimize the impact of what might be *temporarily* very low earnings (due to a recession) or very high earnings (due to a boom), the Shiller CAPE 10 smoothes out earnings by taking the average of the last 10 years' earnings and adjusts that figure for inflation. Let us assume that the Shiller CAPE 10 is at 30 (which it was as we wrote this), well above its historical average. To estimate future returns using this metric, you take the earnings yield — the inverse of the Shiller CAPE 10 ratio — and you get 3.3 percent. However, because the Shiller P/E is based on the lagged 10-year earnings, we need to make an adjustment for the historical growth in real earnings, which is about 1.5 percent per year. To make that adjustment, we then multiply the 3.3 percent earnings yield by 1.075 (.015 x 5), producing an estimated real return to stocks of about 3.5 percent, or 3.4 percentage points below the historical return. (We multiply by five because a 10-year average figure lags current earnings by five years.) Using other methodologies (such as what is called the Gordon Constant Growth Dividend Discount Model) deliver similar results, with most financial economists forecasting real future returns in the range of about 4 to 5 percent.

The second mistake investors make is to treat the expected return as "deterministic" — meaning they believe they will earn that specific return — rather than as just the mean of a potentially very wide dispersion of possible returns. The following illustration demonstrates why thinking of the expected return in a deterministic way is dangerous.

In a November 2012 paper, "An Old Friend: The Stock Market's Shiller PE," Cliff Asness of AQR Capital Management found that the Shiller CAPE 10 does provide valuable information. Specifically, he found that 10-year forward average real returns fall nearly monotonically as starting Shiller P/Es increase. He also found that, as the starting Shiller CAPE 10 increased, worst cases became worse and best cases became weaker. And he found that while the metric provided valuable insights, there were still very wide dispersions of returns. For example:

- When the CAPE 10 was below 9.6, 10-year forward real returns averaged 10.3 percent. In relative terms, that is more than 50 percent above the historical average of 6.8 percent (9.8 percent nominal return less 3.0 percent inflation). The best 10-year forward real return was 17.5 percent. The worst was still a pretty good 4.8 percent 10-year forward real return, just 2.0 percentage points below the average, and 29 percent below it in relative terms. The range between the best and worst outcomes was a 12.7 percentage point difference in real returns.

- When the CAPE 10 was between 15.7 and 17.3 (about its long-term average of 16.5), the 10-year forward real return averaged 5.6 percent. The best and worst 10-year forward real returns were 15.1 percent and 2.3 percent, respectively. The range between the best and worst outcomes was a 12.8 percentage point difference in real returns.

- When the CAPE 10 was between 21.1 and 25.1, the 10-year forward real return averaged just 0.9 percent. The best 10-year forward real return was still 8.3 percent, above the historical average of 6.8 percent. However, the worst 10-year forward real return was now -4.4 percent. The range between the best and worst outcomes was a difference of 12.7 percentage points in real terms.

- When the CAPE 10 was above 25.1, the real return over the following 10 years averaged just 0.5 percent — virtually the same as the long-term real return on the risk-free benchmark, one-month Treasury bills. The best 10-year forward real return was 6.3 percent, just 0.5 percentage points below the historical average. But the worst 10-year forward real return was now -6.1 percent. The range between the best and worst outcomes was a difference of 12.4 percentage points in real terms.

What can we learn from the preceding data? First, starting valuations clearly matter, and they matter a lot. Higher starting values mean that future expected returns are lower, and vice versa. However, a wide

6

dispersion of potential outcomes, for which we must prepare when developing an investment plan, still exists.

The following illustration shows the right way to think about the expected return of a portfolio or an asset class. Although stock returns do not fit exactly into a normal distribution (as the following bell curve depicts), a normal distribution is a close approximation. Thus, we think this graph will be helpful in explaining how to think about expected returns.

In the illustration, think of Portfolio A as a market-like portfolio (such as the Vanguard Total Stock Market Index Fund). Using the 3.5 percent

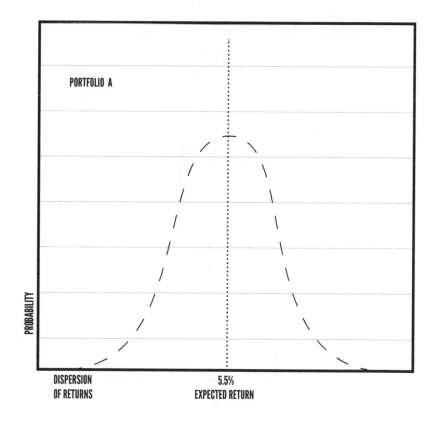

PORTFOLIO A

PROBABILITY

DISPERSION
OF RETURNS

5.5%
EXPECTED RETURN

expected real return to stocks (based on the Shiller CAPE 10) and an expected inflation rate of 2.0 percent, we arrive at an expected nominal return of 5.5 percent for the overall stock market. The right way to think about this 5.5 percent figure is as the mean (and median) of the wide dispersion depicted. In other words, there is a 50 percent chance the actual return will be greater than the expected 5.5 percent, perhaps a 30 percent chance it will be greater than 7 percent, a 10 percent chance it will be greater than 8 percent, and a 5 percent chance it will be greater than 10 percent. The possibilities are similar that it will fall on the left side of the distribution with returns below, and even well below, the expected rate of 5.5 percent.

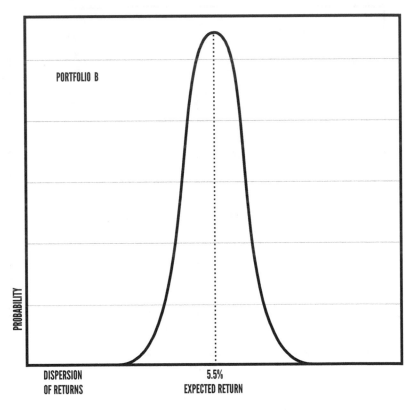

8

Now consider Portfolio B, which has the same 5.5 percent expected return but a different potential dispersion of returns. As the following illustration shows, more of the weight of the distribution (its probability density) is closer to the mean expected return of 5.5 percent than is the case with Portfolio A. It is a taller and thinner bell curve, with less of its weight in the tails, both left (bad) and right (good).

Now consider both Portfolios A and B. They have the same expected return — in both cases the mean return is 5.5 percent. However, they have a different dispersion of returns. If you were faced with the choice of living with the risks of the potential return dispersions in either Portfolio A or B, which would you choose?

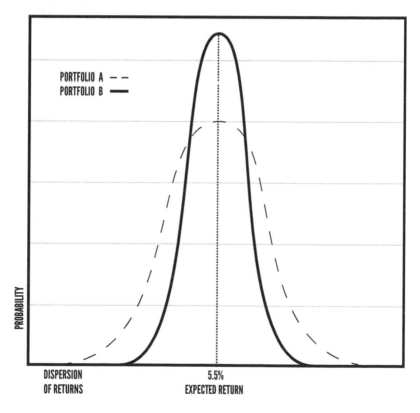

If you are like most people, you would choose to live with the risks of Portfolio B. Most investors are risk averse — given the same expected return, they choose the portfolio with the lower standard deviation of returns (Portfolio B). Said another way, if you are like most investors, you are willing to sacrifice the opportunity to earn the great returns in the right tail of the distribution of Portfolio A (that are not there with Portfolio B) if you also minimize, or eliminate, the risk of the very bad returns in the left tail of Portfolio A (that, again, are not there with Portfolio B).

Are you interested in learning how to create portfolios where the distribution of potential returns looks more like Portfolio B than Portfolio A? Learning how we have been doing this for about 20 years for our clients is the journey we will embark on next, beginning with a history of modern financial theory and asset pricing models.

CHAPTER 2:
A BRIEF HISTORY OF
MODERN FINANCIAL THEORY

The birth of modern finance can be traced back to 1952, when Harry Markowitz's paper "Portfolio Selection" was published in *The Journal of Finance*. The most important aspect of this work was that Markowitz showed it is not a security's own risk and expected return that is important to an investor, but rather the contribution the security makes to the risk and expected return of the investor's entire portfolio. This contribution depends not only on the riskiness of the security itself, but also on how the security behaves relative to the behavior of the other assets in the portfolio (the correlation of their returns). Markowitz was able to show that you could add a risky asset, with higher expected returns, to a portfolio without increasing the portfolio's overall risk if the asset's returns were not perfectly correlated with the other assets in the portfolio.

William Sharpe and John Lintner are typically given most of the credit for introducing the Capital Asset Pricing Model (CAPM). The CAPM was the first formal asset pricing model, and it was built on ideas from

Markowitz's paper. The CAPM provided the first precise definition of risk and how it drives expected returns.

The CAPM looks at returns through a "one-factor" lens, meaning the risk and return of a portfolio is determined only by its exposure to market beta. It is important to understand that market beta is not simply the stock allocation of a portfolio. It is the measure of the equity-type risk of a stock, mutual fund or portfolio relative to the risk of the overall market. An asset (or portfolio) with a market beta greater than 1 has more equity-type risk than the overall market. If it has a market beta less than 1, it has less equity-type risk than the overall market. Thus, a portfolio with a 70 percent allocation to stocks and 30 percent allocation to Treasury bills could have a market beta of 1 if the stocks in the portfolio were highly risky stocks with a market beta of about 1.4. For example, these stocks might be high-flying tech stocks. Conversely, a portfolio with a 100 percent allocation to stocks could have a market beta of just 0.7 if the stocks it held were all less risky than the market as a whole. Perhaps they are "defensive" stocks, such as utilities, drug store chains and supermarket chains.

The CAPM was the finance world's operating model for about 30 years. However, all models by definition are flawed, or wrong. If they were perfectly correct they would be laws, like we have in physics. Over time, anomalies that violated the CAPM began to surface. Among the more prominent ones were:

- 1981: Rolf Banz's "The Relationship Between Return and Market Value of Common Stocks" was published in *The Journal of Financial Economics*. Banz found that market beta does not fully explain the higher average return of small (or lower market capitalization) stocks.

- 1981: Sanjoy Basu's "The Relationship Between Earnings' Yield, Market Value and Return for NYSE Common Stocks," published in *The Journal of Financial Economics*, found that the positive relationship between the earnings yield (the earnings/price ratio) and average return is left unexplained by market beta.

- 1985: Barr Rosenburg, Kenneth Reid and Ronald Lanstein found a positive relationship between average stock return and the book-to-market ratio in their paper "Persuasive Evidence of Market Inefficiency," published in *The Journal of Portfolio Management*.

- 1988: Laxmi Chand Bhandari's "Debt/Equity Ratio and Expected Common Stock Returns: Empirical Evidence," published in *The Journal of Finance*, found that firms with high leverage have higher average returns than firms with low leverage.

Eugene Fama and Kenneth French's 1992 paper "The Cross-Section of Expected Stock Returns" summarized all of these anomalies in one place. The essential conclusions from their paper were that the CAPM only explained about two-thirds of the differences in returns of diversified portfolios, and that a better model could be built using more than just the single factor of market beta.

THE FAMA-FRENCH THREE-FACTOR MODEL

One year later, Fama and French published "Common Risk Factors in the Returns on Stocks and Bonds" in *The Journal of Financial Economics*. This paper proposed a new asset pricing model, called the Fama-French Three-Factor model. This model proposes that, in addition to the market beta factor, exposure to the factors of size and value further explain the cross-section of expected stock returns. The essential takeaway from this research is that small-cap and value stocks are riskier than large-cap and growth stocks, and that risk is compensated for with higher expected returns.

The authors demonstrated that we lived not in a one-factor world, but in a three-factor world. In so doing, they showed how the risk and expected return of a portfolio is explained by not only its exposure to market beta, but also by its exposure to the size (small stocks) and price (stocks with low prices relative to book value, or value stocks) factors. Fama and French hypothesized that while small-cap and value stocks have higher market betas — more equity-type risk — they also contain additional, unique risks unrelated to market beta. Thus, small-cap and value stocks are riskier than large-cap and growth stocks, explaining their higher historical returns and implying that such stocks should have higher expected returns in the future. Studies have confirmed that the three-factor model explains an overwhelming majority of the returns of diversified portfolios. In fact, the Fama-French three-factor model improved the explanatory power from about two-thirds of the differences in returns between diversified portfolios to more than 90 percent. An indirect, but important, implication of this finding was that if more than 90 percent of a diversified portfolio's returns could be explained by the portfolio's exposure to these factors, there wasn't much room left for active security selection or market timing to add value. This suggests, in turn, that passive, evidence-based investing is the strategy most likely to allow you to achieve your financial goals. Subsequent research on active managers' performance and persistence of performance supports that conclusion.

THE THREE FACTORS

Before looking at the returns to the market beta, size and value factors, we need to go over a few key points. The first is that factor returns are always expressed in terms of *annual average* returns, not compound or *annualized* returns. If we have 90 years of data, we calculate a factor's return over that period by taking the sum of the returns in each of those 90 years and dividing the total by 90. The second point is that factors are always considered long-short portfolios. Thus:

- The market beta factor is the *average annual* return on the total stock market (the long) *minus* the *average annual* return on Treasury bills (the short). From 1927 through 2016, the *average annual* return of market beta has been 8.4 percent.

- The size factor is the *annual average* return on small-cap stocks (the long) *minus* the *average annual* return on large-cap stocks (the short). Using the Center for Research in Securities Prices at the University of Chicago (CRSP) data, small stocks are those in deciles 6-10 of all stocks sorted by market capitalization and large stocks are those in deciles 1-5. From 1927 through 2016, small-cap companies have outperformed large-cap companies by an annual average of 3.3 percent per year.

- The value (or price) factor is the *average annual* return on value stocks (the long) *minus* the *average annual* return on growth stocks (the short). Ranking stocks by their book-to-market values, value stocks are the 30 percent of stocks with the highest book-to-market values and growth stocks are the 30 percent with the lowest book-to-market values. From 1927 through 2016, value companies have outperformed growth companies by an annual average of 5.1 percent per year.

INDEPENDENT RISK FACTORS

An important contribution Fama and French made to the evolution of asset pricing models was to show that size and price (value) are independent (unique) risk factors in that they give investors exposure to different risks than exposure to market risk (market beta) does. Evidence of this independence can be seen when we examine the historical correlations of the size and price factors to the market factor. High correlations would mean the risk factors would be relatively good substitutes for each other. If that were the case, while investors could increase the expected return (and risk) of their portfolio by increasing their exposure to these risk factors, there would be little real diversification benefit. If the correlations are low, investors could both increase expected returns for a given level of risk and gain a diversification benefit. Thus, finding factors with low correlation provides valuable information we can use to build more efficient portfolios.

Because most people have an incorrect understanding of the term correlation (even many of the professional advisors we have met), before exploring the data we need to make sure you know and fully comprehend the definitions of positive and negative correlation.

A positive correlation exists between two assets when one asset produces above-average returns (relative to its average) and the other asset *tends* to also produce above-average returns (relative to its average). The stronger the tendency, the closer the correlation will be to +1.

While most people seem to believe negative correlation means that when one asset increases in value the other falls in value, it actually means that when one asset produces above-average returns (relative to its average), the other asset *tends* to produce below-average returns (relative to its average). The stronger the tendency, the closer the correlation will be to -1.

If the correlation is 0, two assets would be said to be uncorrelated. That means that when one asset produces above average-returns relative to its average, the other asset is just as likely to also produce above-average returns relative to its average as it is likely to produce below-average returns relative to its average.

Some examples will help clarify this concept.

Example 1:

Consider two assets, A and B, and their returns over a 10-year period. Their return series is depicted in the following table.

ASSET	YEAR 1	YEAR 2	YEAR 3	YEAR 4	YEAR 5	YEAR 6	YEAR 7	YEAR 8	YEAR 9	YEAR 10
A	12%	8%	12%	8%	12%	8%	12%	8%	12%	8%
B	8%	12%	8%	12%	8%	12%	8%	12%	8%	12%

Both assets A and B have an annual average return of 10 percent. Whenever A's return is above its average of 10 percent, B's return is below its average of 10 percent. And whenever A's return is below its average of 10 percent, B's return is above its average of 10 percent. Thus, the assets are negatively correlated. Note that they are negatively correlated even though they both always produce positive returns.

Example 2:

ASSET	YEAR 1	YEAR 2	YEAR 3	YEAR 4	YEAR 5	YEAR 6	YEAR 7	YEAR 8	YEAR 9	YEAR 10
A	2%	-2%	2%	-2%	2%	-2%	2%	-2%	2%	-2%
B	-2%	2%	-2%	2%	-2%	2%	-2%	2%	-2%	2%

Both assets A and B in this series have an average annual return of 0 percent. Whenever A's return is above its average of 0 percent, B's return is below its average of 0 percent. And whenever A's return is below its average of 0 percent, B's return is above its average of 0 percent. Thus, again we see that the two assets are negatively correlated.

Now comes the fun part. We will string together the two examples so that we have a 20-year period. The first 10 years are the returns from Example 1, and the second 10 years are from Example 2. Thus, the return series looks like this:

Asset A: 12, 8, 12, 8, 12, 8, 12, 8, 12, 8, 2, -2, 2, -2, 2, -2, 2, -2, 2, -2
Asset B: 8, 12, 8, 12, 8, 12, 8, 12, 8, 12, -2, 2, -2, 2, -2, 2, -2, 2, -2, 2

Recall that both A and B had average returns in the first 10 years of 10 percent, and average returns of 0 percent in the second 10 years. Thus, their average return for the full 20 years in both cases is 5 percent. Now, recall our definitions. If you are not sure, go back and read them again before attempting to answer this question: Are A and B positively or negatively correlated?

With the definitions in mind, we see that whenever A's return was above its average of 5 percent, B's return was also above its average of 5 percent. And whenever A's return was below its average of 5 percent, B's return was also below its average of 5 percent. Thus, we see that, despite the fact A and B were negatively correlated over each of the two 10-year sub-periods, over the full 20-year period they were positively correlated. Besides illustrating the concepts of positive and negative correlation, we hope you also come away with the understanding that you need long-term data series for correlations to have any real meaning. In addition, it is important to understand that correlations of risky assets have a tendency to drift over time. As 2008 demonstrated, the correlation of all risky assets has a nasty tendency to move toward 1 during crises. Thus, when considering an asset for inclusion in a portfolio, you need not only to think about the asset's long-term correlation with other portfolio assets, but also when the correlation tends to rise and when it tends to fall.

With these important understandings, we now turn to examining the long-term correlation of the three Fama-French factors. The following data shows the annual correlations of returns to the market beta, size and value factors from 1927 through 2016.

	MARKET BETA	SIZE	VALUE
MARKET BETA	1.0	0.3	-0.2
SIZE	0.3	1.0	0.0
VALUE	-0.2	0.0	1.0

What we find is that the size factor has a correlation of about 0.3 to market beta. Recalling our definitions, there is a tendency, though not a very strong one, that whenever the market beta factor (the return of stocks minus the return of one-month Treasury bills) produces a return greater than 8.4 percent (its average premium), small-cap stocks will outperform large-cap stocks by more than the average premium of 3.3 percent a year. On the other hand, there will also be a significant number of years when the return on market beta is greater than its average of 8.4 percent and the size premium will be below 3.3 percent, including many years when the size premium will be negative (large-cap stocks will outperform small-cap stocks).

We also see that the value factor has a correlation to the market beta factor of -0.2. Again recalling our definitions, whenever the market beta factor is greater than 8.4 percent, there is a small tendency for the value premium to be less than its average of 5.1 percent, and vice versa.

Finally, the correlation of the size factor to the value factor was 0.0 — their returns are uncorrelated. Thus, when the size premium is greater than its average of 3.3 percent, the value premium is just as likely to be greater than its average of 5.1 percent as it is to be below it.

The low to negative correlations of these factors become apparent when we look at their returns in 1998 and 2001. The following table shows the returns of the S&P 500 Index and two Dimensional Fund Advisors (DFA) asset class mutual funds, the DFA U.S. Small Cap Portfolio and the DFA U.S. Small Cap Value Portfolio. The table also shows the return of a portfolio holding one-third of its assets in each of the three.

	S&P 500 INDEX	DFA U.S. SMALL CAP PORTFOLIO	DFA U.S. SMALL CAP VALUE PORTFOLIO	EQUAL-WEIGHTED PORTFOLIO
1998	28.6	-5.5	-7.3	5.3
2001	-11.9	12.7	22.7	7.8

Note that the gap between the good and bad years was 40.5 percentage points for the S&P 500 Index, 18.2 percentage points for the DFA U.S. Small Cap Portfolio and 30 percentage points for the DFA U.S. Small Cap Value Portfolio, but just 2.5 percentage points for the equal-weighted portfolio. This simple example conveys the benefits of diversifying across factors that have low correlation — you dampen the volatility of the portfolio. Dampening volatility is especially important to those in the withdrawal phase of their investment lifecycle, when the order of returns matters a great deal because higher volatility can greatly affect the odds of outliving your assets.

The bottom line is that our three Fama-French factors have low correlations to each other. In fact, the size and value factors have been uncorrelated (their correlation was 0). That is good news, which we will use to build more efficient portfolios.

ACHIEVING YOUR GOALS IN A CAPM WORLD

In a CAPM (or one-factor) framework, the only ways to increase the expected return of your portfolio are to increase your allocation to stocks or to purchase higher-market-beta stocks. In either case, you are not diversifying the sources of the portfolio's return — just adding more market beta to it.

An example can illustrate this point. Let's assume equities (as represented by a total stock market fund) are expected to return 7 percent and bonds (as represented by the yield on, say, a five-year Treasury bond) are expected to return 5 percent. We'll use these figures to keep the math simple. Based upon your ability and willingness to take risk, you decide that a portfolio with an allocation of 50 percent stocks and 50 percent bonds would be appropriate. Such a portfolio would have an expected return of 6 percent. However, the desired spending component of your long-term financial plan requires a 6.5 percent return. In a one-factor world, to achieve the expected return of 6.5 percent, you have to increase your equity allocation to 75 percent.

Portfolio 1: (75% x 7%) + (25% x 5%) = 6.5%

The only other alternative would be to increase the market beta of the stocks in your portfolio. The math works out in such a way that you would be left owning a portfolio consisting basically of only very high-market-beta stocks. In either case, you would be adding more of the same market beta risk already in your portfolio. Instead putting all your eggs in one risk basket (market beta), would it not be better to diversify your sources of risk across other baskets with unique risks? Another important consideration is that the portfolio with 75 percent stocks is riskier than the one with just 50 percent stocks — the allocation you felt was appropriate based on your risk tolerance.

ACHIEVING YOUR GOALS
IN A THREE-FACTOR WORLD

The science of investing offers an alternative way to increase the expected return of your portfolio. Since 1927, small value stocks have outperformed the market (as represented by the S&P 500 Index) by an *annualized* 3.8 percentage points. Thus, if we assume stocks will return 7 percent, we might assume small value stocks will return an additional 3.8 percentage points a year for a total return of 10.8 percent.

Recall our initial example of a 50 percent stock/50 percent bond allocation. Instead of increasing your stock allocation to achieve the higher 6.5 percent return, you decide to divide your 50 percent stock allocation equally between the S&P 500 Index and small value stocks — 25 percent each. Now the expected return is almost 7 percent.

Portfolio 2: (25% x 7%) + (25% x 10.8%) + (50% x 5%) = 6.95%

Without increasing your stock allocation, you have increased the portfolio's expected return to more than the required 6.5 percent. We did this by adding an allocation to the higher expected returning small value stocks. It is important to recognize that while your exposure to stocks basically remained unchanged (the allocation of small value stocks, while riskier, did add two new unique risk factors, providing some diversification benefit), the expected return of the portfolio increased by more than the risk (the expected standard deviation of return). However, you don't need to earn 6.95 percent. Your plan only requires a return of 6.5 percent. With that in mind, we can try lowering the stock allocation to 40 percent, again splitting it equally between the S&P 500 Index and small value stocks. Now the expected return is:

Portfolio 3: (20% x 7%) + (20% x 10.8%) + (60% x 5%) = 6.56%

You have now achieved your goal of an expected return of 6.5 percent. And you did so with an allocation to stocks of only 40 percent. Using your intuition, which portfolio, Portfolio 1 or Portfolio 3, do you think is riskier? Which portfolio would you expect to perform worse in a bear market? Intuitively, most people will say Portfolio 1.

While Portfolio 3 has the same expected return as the 75 percent equity portfolio, the risks are completely different. Portfolios with higher equity allocations have greater potential for losses. The tradeoff is that the potential upside of the portfolios with higher equity allocations is much greater. For investors for whom the pain of a loss is greater than the benefit of an equal-sized gain (probably you), reducing downside risk as the price of reducing upside potential is a good tradeoff.

Let's tackle another consideration especially important to loss-averse investors (which most are). Because bonds are safer investments than stocks, in a severe bear market the portfolio's maximum loss would likely be far lower with a 40 percent equity allocation than with a 75 percent one. 2008 provided a great example, at least if the fixed income investments you owned were limited to Treasuries and other high-quality bonds. While the market fell 37 percent, five-year Treasury bonds rose about 13 percent. And Portfolio 3 not only owned less of the losing stocks, but far more of the winning bonds.

Using the S&P 500 Index, the Russell 2000 Value Index (for small-cap value stocks) and the five-year Treasury, we see that in 2008, Portfolio 1 would have lost 24.5 percent, Portfolio 2 would have lost 9.9 percent and Portfolio 3 would have lost just 5.3 percent.

Thus, while the expected returns of Portfolio 1 and Portfolio 3 are the same, the portfolio with the lower equity allocation has much less downside risk. Of course, the upside potential during a strong bull market is correspondingly lower. For example, in 2003, Portfolio 1 gained 35.1 percent, Portfolio 2 gained 19.9 percent and Portfolio 3 gained just 16.4 percent.

To illustrate why reducing downside risk at the price of limiting upside potential is likely a good tradeoff, examine the chart below.

As you can see in the illustration on the next page, Portfolio 1 experienced more years in which returns fall on the left-hand side of the chart, as well as more years in which they fall on the right-hand side of the chart — the tails were bigger.

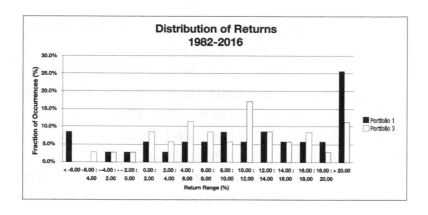

CONSIDERATIONS

When constructing a portfolio — deciding on the right asset allocation — you should carefully consider several factors. For example, you should consider how your labor capital correlates with the greater economic cycle risks of small-cap and value stocks compared to large-cap and growth stocks.

Another important consideration is a psychological one referred to as the risk of tracking error regret. Tracking error is the amount by which a portfolio's performance varies from that of the total market or other broad market benchmark, such as the S&P 500 Index. By diversifying across risk factors, investors take on increased tracking error regret risk because their portfolios look less like the market. While very few investors care when tracking error is positive (their portfolio beats the benchmark), many care very much when it is negative. Misery loves company. In other words, if your portfolio performs poorly because "the market" has performed poorly, at least you have company. On the other hand, if your portfolio is underperforming the market, you might begin to question your strategy, wondering why you are doing relatively poorly.

1998 provided the perfect example of this, as the DFA Small Value Portfolio underperformed the S&P 500 Index by about 36 percentage points. Such underperformance can test the mettle of even the most disciplined investors. Compounding the problem is that, to adhere to your asset allocation plan, you would be required to rebalance the portfolio — selling some of the S&P 500 Index allocation (having just seen it gain almost 29 percent) to buy some of the poorly performing DFA Small Value Portfolio (which just lost more than 7 percent). Because most investors chase returns, they would be far more likely to increase their allocation to the S&P 500 Index and get rid of their small value allocation. Of course, doing so would be pursuing a strategy of buying high and selling low — not exactly a prescription for investment success. It is why the evidence shows that investors, on average, underperform the very mutual funds in which they invest. On the other hand, investors who remained disciplined and rebalanced would have bought more small value stocks at low prices and sold some of their S&P 500 Index holdings at high prices, a far more successful strategy. It also would have left them much better prepared for 2001, because they already would have sold some of their S&P 500 Index holdings (which performed poorly then) and increased their small value holdings (which performed well).

The bottom line is that, to have a chance to benefit from positive tracking error, investors must accept the virtual certainty that negative tracking error will appear from time to time. Emotions associated with negative tracking error can lead investors to abandon carefully developed investment plans. Only investors willing and able to accept the risk of tracking error regret should consider diversifying across other risk factors.

In the next chapter, we will show you how you can utilize what you have learned to build more efficient portfolios by combining Fama and French's work with insights from Harry Markowitz's work that won a

Nobel Prize. We will explain how you can add risky, but non-perfectly correlating, assets to a portfolio and generate higher returns without a commensurate increase in the portfolio's volatility.

CHAPTER 3:
BUILDING A MORE
EFFICIENT PORTFOLIO

We will begin with a portfolio that has a conventional asset allocation of 60 percent stocks and 40 percent bonds. In this case, the stock allocation is to the S&P 500 Index and the bond allocation is to five-year Treasury notes (the highest quality intermediate-term bond). The time frame will be the 42-year period from 1975 through 2016. We chose this period because it is the longest for which we have data on the indices we need. While maintaining the same 60 percent stock/40 percent bond allocation, we will then expand our investment universe to include equity asset classes other than U.S. large-cap stocks. We will see how the portfolio performed if one had the patience to stay with this allocation for the duration and rebalanced annually. We will then demonstrate how the portfolio's performance could have been made more efficient by increasing its diversification across asset classes. We do so in four simple steps. (Indices are not available for direct investment.)

PORTFOLIO 1

S&P 500 Index   60%

Five-Year Treasury Notes*   40%

1975–2016

ANNUALIZED RETURN (%)	ANNUAL STANDARD DEVIATION (%)
10.4	10.3

*Data source: © 2017 Morningstar, Inc. All rights reserved. Reproduced with permission.

By changing the composition of the control portfolio, we will see how we can improve its efficiency. To avoid being accused of data mining, we will alter our allocations by arbitrarily "cutting things in half."

Step 1: The first step is to diversify our stock holdings to include an allocation to U.S. small-cap stocks. Therefore, we reduce our allocation to the S&P 500 Index from 60 percent to 30 percent and allocate 30 percent to the Fama/French US Small Cap Index. (The Fama-French indices use the academic definitions of asset classes. Note that regulated utilities have been excluded from the data.)

PORTFOLIO 2

S&P 500 Index   30%

Fama/French US Small Cap Index   30%

Five-Year Treasury Notes*   40%

1975–2016

	ANNUALIZED RETURN (%)	ANNUAL STANDARD DEVIATION (%)
PORTFOLIO 1	10.4	10.3
PORTFOLIO 2	11.5	11.0

Step 2: Our next step is to diversify our domestic stock holdings to include value stocks. We shift half of our 30 percent allocation to the S&P 500 Index to a large-cap value index and half of our 30 percent allocation to small-cap stocks to a small-cap value index.

PORTFOLIO 3

S&P 500 Index	15%
Fama/French US Large Value Index (ex utilities)	15%
Fama/French US Small Cap Index	15%
Fama/French US Small Value Index (ex utilities)	15%
Five-Year Treasury Notes*	40%

1975–2016

	ANNUALIZED RETURN (%)	ANNUAL STANDARD DEVIATION (%)
PORTFOLIO 1	10.4	10.3
PORTFOLIO 2	11.5	11.0
PORTFOLIO 3	12.0	12.2

Step 3: Our next step is to shift half of our equity allocation to international stocks. For exposure to international value and international small-cap stocks, we will add a 15 percent allocation to both the MSCI EAFE Value Index and the Dimensional International Small Cap Index.

PORTFOLIO 4

S&P 500 Index	7.5%
Fama/French US Large Value Index (ex utilities)	7.5%
Fama/French US Small Cap Index	7.5%
Fama/French US Small Value Index (ex utilities)	7.5%
MSCI EAFE Value Index*	15%
Dimensional International Small Cap Index	15%
Five-Year Treasury Notes**	40%

1975–2016

	ANNUALIZED RETURN (%)	ANNUAL STANDARD DEVIATION (%)
PORTFOLIO 1	10.4	10.3
PORTFOLIO 2	11.5	11.0
PORTFOLIO 3	12.0	12.2
PORTFOLIO 4	11.8	11.4

*Data source: MSCI

**Data source: © 2017 Morningstar, Inc. All rights reserved. Reproduced with permission.

One effect of the changes has been to increase the return on the portfolio from 10.4 percent to 11.8 percent. This outcome is what we should have expected to see as we added riskier small-cap and value stocks to our portfolio. Thus, we also need to consider how our changes impacted the risk of the portfolio. The standard deviation (a measure of volatility, or risk) of the portfolio increased from 10.3 percent to 11.4 percent. Returns increased by a relative 13.5 percent while the relative increase in volatility was 10.7 percent.

You have now observed the power of modern portfolio theory at work. You saw how you can add risky (and, therefore, higher expected returning) assets to a portfolio and increase its returns more than its risk rose. That is the benefit of diversification across asset classes that are not perfectly correlated. While most investors and advisors with this knowledge have used it in the preceding manner, there is another way to consider employing it. Instead of trying to increase returns without proportionally increasing risk, we can try to achieve the same return while lowering the risk of the portfolio. To achieve this goal, we increase the bond allocation from 40 percent to 60 percent and proportionally decrease the allocations to each of the equity asset classes.

PORTFOLIO 5

S&P 500 Index	5%
Fama/French US Large Value Index (ex utilities)	5%
Fama/French US Small Cap Index	5%
Fama/French US Small Value Index (ex utilities)	5%
MSCI EAFE Value Index*	10%
Dimensional International Small Cap Index	10%
Five-Year Treasury Notes**	60%

1975–2016

	ANNUALIZED RETURN (%)	ANNUAL STANDARD DEVIATION (%)
PORTFOLIO 1	10.4	10.3
PORTFOLIO 2	11.5	11.0
PORTFOLIO 3	12.0	12.2
PORTFOLIO 4	11.8	11.4
PORTFOLIO 5	10.4	8.2

*Data source: MSCI

**Data source: © 2017 Morningstar, Inc. All rights reserved. Reproduced with permission.

Compared with Portfolio 1, Portfolio 5 achieved the same return with far less risk. Specifically, Portfolio 5 returned the exact same 10.4 percent per year while experiencing volatility 2.1 percentage points lower (8.2 percent versus 10.3 percent). In relative terms, its volatility was 20.4 percent lower.

Now that you have a good understanding of how modern portfolio theory can be used to build more efficient portfolios, we will move to our last step. We will show you how, by concentrating your equity allocation in only the highest expected returning asset classes, you can improve a portfolio's risk profile even further, making it look more like Portfolio B (the one you preferred) than Portfolio A from the illustration in Chapter 1.

Just as the equity premium is compensation for taking risk, so are the size and value premiums. Thus, we add the usual disclaimer that the future may look different from the past. There are no guarantees in investing.

Due to data limitations, the period we will now consider is the 35 years from 1982 through 2016. We will look at two portfolios, A and B.

Portfolio A is again allocated 60 percent to the S&P 500 Index and 40 percent to five-year Treasury notes. Portfolio B will hold 25 percent stocks and 75 percent five-year Treasury notes. With U.S. stocks representing roughly half of the global equity market capitalization, we will split the equity allocation equally between U.S. small value stocks (using the Fama/French US Small Value Index) and international small value stocks (using the Dimensional International Small Cap Value Index).

1982–2016

	PORTFOLIO A	PORTFOLIO B
ANNUALIZED RETURNS/STANDARD DEVIATION (%)	10.3/10.3	9.7/7.2
YEARS WITH RETURNS ABOVE 15%/BELOW -15%	11/1	9/0
YEARS WITH RETURNS ABOVE 20%/BELOW -20%	7/0	2/0
YEARS WITH RETURNS ABOVE 25%/-25%	2/0	2/0
WORST YEAR RETURN/BEST YEAR RETURN (%)	-17.0/29.3	-1.4/28.0
NUMBER OF YEARS WITH NEGATIVE RETURN	5	3

Portfolio A: 60 percent S&P 500 Index/40 percent five-year Treasury notes*

Portfolio B: 12.5 percent Fama/French US Small Value Index (ex utilities)/12.5 percent Dimensional International Small Cap Value Index/75 percent five-year Treasury notes*

*Data source: © 2017 Morningstar, Inc. All rights reserved. Reproduced with permission.

As you can see, while Portfolio A produced an annualized return 0.6 percentage points higher than Portfolio B (10.3 percent versus 9.7 percent), it did so while experiencing volatility 3.1 percentage points greater (10.3 percent versus 7.2 percent). In relative terms, Portfolio A's annualized return was only 6 percent greater than Portfolio B's while the volatility it experienced was 43 percent higher. In addition, Portfolio B had fewer events in the tails of the return distribution (said another way, it had both fewer extremely good and fewer extremely bad years). While

Portfolio A had 11 years with returns greater than 15 percent, Portfolio B had nine. And while Portfolio A had one year with a loss greater than 15 percent, Portfolio B never experienced one that large. Moving the hurdle to years with 20 percent gains or losses, we see that Portfolio A had seven years with returns greater than that level and no years with losses of that size while Portfolio B had just two years of gains that large. Moving the hurdle to the 25 percent level, both Portfolio A and Portfolio B had two years with returns in excess of that amount and no years with losses that great. The best single year for Portfolio A was 1995, when it returned 29.3 percent. The best single year for Portfolio B was 1985, when it returned 28.0 percent. Note that while Portfolio B has just 25 percent in equities, its best year was almost as good as the best year for Portfolio A, which has 60 percent in equities. On the other hand, Portfolio A's worst single year was 2008, when it lost 17.0 percent. The worst single year for Portfolio B was 1994, when it lost just 1.2 percent. In addition, while Portfolio A experienced five years of negative returns, Portfolio B posted just three.

Portfolio B — the low-market-beta/high-tilt portfolio — with its shorter tails looks more like our original Portfolio B. While its best year was not as good as Portfolio A's best year, and it had fewer years in the good right tail, its worst year was much less painful than Portfolio A's worst year, and it had fewer years in the bad right tail.

There is another important point to cover, and to help make it we have reproduced the original illustration of the potential dispersion of returns for Portfolios A and B on the next page.

Recall your preference for Portfolio B was based on your aversion to risk — your willingness to give up the opportunity for the extreme good returns in the right tail of Portfolio A in return for minimizing the risks of the extreme bad returns in its left tail. The illustration shows that, if you

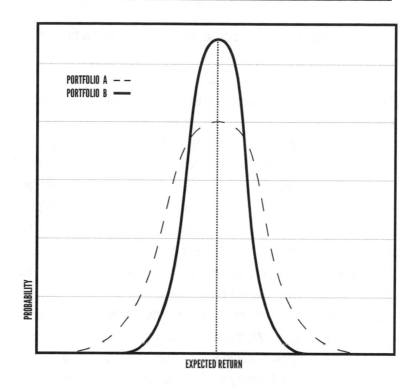

choose Portfolio B, both the good and bad tails of Portfolio A are reduced equally. However, using actual returns, we saw that while Portfolio A did produce more good years than Portfolio B, and had a higher best returning year than Portfolio B, the difference in returns between their best years was just 1 percentage point while the difference in returns between their worst years was almost 16 percentage points. In other words, bad tail risk was curtailed much more than good tail risk. If you preferred Portfolio B to Portfolio A, you should have a strong preference for a low-market-beta/high-tilt portfolio.

Before moving on, we must admit there is no way that, in 1982, we could have predicted the allocation for Portfolio B would have produced returns so similar to the allocation for Portfolio A. We might have guessed at a similar allocation, but we cannot predict the future with anything close to that kind of accuracy.

We have one final example to take you through. On December 23, 2011, Ron Lieber, financial columnist for *The New York Times*, wrote an article titled "Taking a Chance on the Larry Portfolio" — and the "Larry Portfolio" (LP) was born. The LP is the "technical" term for a portfolio that basically limits its stock holdings to the highest returning equity asset classes available to individual investors in low-cost, passively managed investment vehicles, specifically U.S. small value stocks, developed markets small value stocks and emerging market value stocks. Limiting stock holdings to the highest expected returning asset classes allows you to maintain a lower overall allocation to stocks and achieve the same expected return in your portfolio.

Due to data limitations, we now will consider the 28-year period from 1989 through 2016. We will again look at two portfolios, A and B. Portfolio A is once again allocated 60 percent to the S&P 500 Index and 40 percent to five-year Treasury notes. Portfolio B will hold 28 percent stocks and 72 percent five-year Treasury notes. (Note the change from the previous example, which used 25 percent stocks, and recall our disclaimer that we cannot predict with perfect accuracy what allocation will produce the same returns.) Again we split our equity holdings, with domestic and international stocks each receiving a 14 percent allocation. Emerging market stocks make up about 25 percent of international equity capitalization, so our international allocation becomes 10.5 percent international small value stocks and 3.5 percent emerging markets value stocks (using the Fama/French Emerging Markets Value Index).

1989-2016

	PORTFOLIO A	PORTFOLIO B
ANNUALIZED RETURNS/STANDARD DEVIATION (%)	8.9/10.5	8.3/6.7
YEARS WITH RETURNS ABOVE 15%/BELOW -15%	7/1	6/0
YEARS WITH RETURNS ABOVE 20%/BELOW -20%	5/0	1/0
YEARS WITH RETURNS ABOVE 25%/-25%	1/0	0/0
WORST YEAR RETURN/BEST YEAR RETURN (%)	-17.0/29.3	-3.3/22.2
NUMBER OF YEARS WITH NEGATIVE RETURN	5	3

Portfolio A: 60 percent S&P 500 Index/40 percent five-year Treasury notes*

Portfolio B: 14 percent Fama/French US Small Value Index (ex utilities)/10.5 percent Dimensional International Small Cap Value Index/3.5 percent Fama/French Emerging Markets Value Index /72 percent five-year Treasury notes*

*Data source: © 2017 Morningstar, Inc. All rights reserved. Reproduced with permission.

Portfolio A produced an annualized return 0.6 percentage points higher than Portfolio B (8.9 percent versus 8.3 percent), but it did so with volatility 3.8 percentage points greater (10.5 percent versus 6.7 percent). In relative terms, Portfolio A's annualized return was only 7 percent greater than Portfolio B's, while the volatility it experienced was 57 percent greater higher. In addition, Portfolio B generally had fewer events in the tails (fewer extremely good and fewer extremely bad years). Portfolio A had seven years with returns greater than 15 percent while Portfolio B had six. However, while Portfolio A had one year with a loss greater than 15 percent, Portfolio B never experienced one that large. Moving the hurdle to years with 20 percent gains or losses, we see that Portfolio A had five years with returns greater than that level and no years with losses of that size while Portfolio B had just one year of returns that large. Moving the hurdle to the 25 percent level, Portfolio

A had one year with a return in excess of that amount and no years with losses that great. Portfolio B did not experience a single year with a loss or gain of 25 percent or greater. The best single year for Portfolio A was 1995, when it returned 29.3 percent. The best single year for Portfolio B was 2003, when it returned 22.2 percent. Note that while Portfolio B has just 28 percent in equities, its best year's return was only 7.1 percentage points lower than Portfolio A's best year. On the other hand, in 2008, the worst year for both portfolios, Portfolio B lost just 3.3 percent, 13.7 percentage points less than Portfolio A's loss of 17.0 percent. In addition, while Portfolio A experienced five years of negative returns, Portfolio B recorded just three. If you are like most investors, you would have slept much better with Portfolio B than with Portfolio A.

Experience has taught us that limiting the risk of large losses increases the odds that you will be able to maintain discipline during bear markets, thereby avoiding the panicked selling that destroys the odds of achieving your financial goals.

The next chapter addresses a question we are often asked: Is the "Larry Portfolio" well diversified?

CHAPTER 4:
IS THE "LARRY PORTFOLIO"
WELL DIVERSIFIED?

While the "Larry Portfolio" (LP) has earned superior risk-adjusted returns (producing a higher Sharpe ratio than a market-like portfolio, with much smaller worst-case losses) over the 28-year period we examined, one concern investors have expressed is that the portfolio "is not well diversified."[1] In one sense that is a true statement. The LP does limit its stock holdings in both the U.S. and developed international markets to small value stocks, and in emerging markets to value stocks. That means it holds no small-cap, mid-cap and large-cap growth companies in the U.S. and developed international markets, as well as no mid-cap and large-cap value companies. In emerging markets, there are no growth stocks, just value stocks.

To answer the question of whether the LP is well diversified, we need to have you think about diversification differently from the way you

---

[1] Past performance is not a guarantee of future results.

probably are used to. The conventional way of addressing how well a portfolio is diversified is to think in terms of the number and weighting of individual stocks, asset classes and geographic regions. We want you to also think about diversification in terms of exposure to the factors that determine the risk and return of a portfolio.

As we have discussed, to understand how markets work, financial economists have developed what are called asset pricing (factor) models. Until recently, the "workhorse" model was the Fama-French three-factor model. Again, the model's three factors are market beta (exposure to the risk of the stock market), size (exposure to the risk of small-cap stocks) and value (exposure to the risk of value stocks). To determine how well a highly tilted portfolio is diversified, we will begin by looking at the exposure a total stock market fund (portfolio) has to the three Fama-French factors.

A total stock market (TSM) fund has, by definition, an exposure to market beta of 1. However, while a TSM fund holds small stocks, it has no exposure at all to the size factor. This seeming contradiction confuses many investors. The confusion arises because factors are long/short portfolios. The size factor is the return of small-cap stocks *minus* the return of large-cap stocks. In other words, small-cap stocks provide a *positive* exposure to the size effect and large-cap stocks provide a *negative* exposure to it. Thus, while the small-cap stocks in a TSM fund provide *positive* exposure to the size factor, the large-cap stocks in the fund provide an exactly offsetting amount of *negative* exposure. That puts the *net* exposure to the size factor at 0. The same is true for value stocks. The value factor is the return of value stocks minus the return of growth stocks. Value stocks provide a *positive* exposure to the value effect and growth stocks a *negative* exposure. While the value stocks in a TSM fund provide *positive* exposure to the value factor, the growth stocks in the fund provide an exactly offsetting amount of *negative* exposure. That puts the *net* exposure to the value factor at 0.

We now turn to the LP's factor exposure. The funds we use to build the LP create an end portfolio with loadings on (or exposure to) the size and value factors of approximately 0.6. However, the exact amounts depend on which funds are used to implement the strategy because different funds in the same asset class (in this case small value) can have different exposures to the size and value factors. The smaller the weighted average market capitalization of the stocks in the fund, and the lower their weighted average price-to-book ratio, the greater the exposure to the factors will be. Like most well-diversified stock portfolios, its equity portion has a market beta of about 1.

Now consider a portfolio that uses the LP's high-tilt, low-market-beta approach and has a 30 percent allocation to stocks. The portfolio will have a market beta of about 0.3 (1 x 0.3), a size loading of about 0.18 (0.6 x 0.3) and a value loading of about 0.18 (0.6 x 0.3). The portfolio's bond holdings will also give it exposure to term risk, another factor. How much will depend on the maturity of the bonds used for the portfolio's fixed income portion. The portfolio therefore has exposure to four factors, each of which has a low to negative correlation with the other factors. Contrast that with a TSM portfolio fully allocated to stocks. It has a market beta of 1, and that is the only factor to which it is exposed.

Thus, while a TSM fund is more diversified when you think about diversification across asset classes (it holds more equity asset classes/fills in more of Morningstar's style boxes), the LP is more diversified when looking at exposure to risk factors. A TSM fund has all of its eggs in one risk basket — market beta — while the LP diversifies its risks across three stock risk baskets: market beta, size and value, as well as the term factor in its bond holdings. The LP is also just as diversified in terms of economic and geopolitical risks across countries. And it certainly holds a sufficient number of stocks. Using international small-cap value and emerging market value funds from Dimensional Fund Advisors and Bridgeway's Omni Small Value Fund, the LP holds the stocks of about 5,100 companies from 42 countries — certainly more than enough to diversify away any idiosyncratic risks. In fact, it contains not that many fewer stocks than Vanguard's Total World Stock Index Fund, which holds about 7,800 stocks also from 42 countries.

The bottom line is that the LP is well-diversified, just not so much when it's thought about in terms of a traditional *asset class* approach. And while this leaves the investor subject to that dreaded psychological disease known as tracking error regret — the portfolio's returns will look very different from those of the market — the benefits in terms of reduced tail risk are large in comparison.

SUPPORT FOR FACTOR DIVERSIFICATION

Louis Scott and Stefano Cavaglia, authors of the study "A Wealth Management Perspective on Factor Premia and the Value of Downside Protection," published in the Spring 2017 issue of *The Journal of Portfolio Management*, provide support for the benefits of factor diversification. The focus of their study, which examined four factors (the Fama-French size and value factors as well as the two newer momentum and quality factors), was to determine if factor diversification improved terminal wealth and the odds of retirees in the withdrawal phase of their investment cycle not outliving their portfolios.

To test their hypothesis, Scott and Cavaglia considered a baseline investment strategy comprising a passive, fully invested exposure to global equities (the MSCI World Index) over a 20-year horizon. They then examined the effect of adding an overlay of factor premiums on the distribution of terminal wealth. They used utility functions to quantify the hedging benefits of factor premiums to the baseline investment strategy. Their dataset covers the period from November 1990 through December 2012.

Momentum is the tendency for assets that have performed well (poorly) in the recent past to continue to perform well (poorly) in the future, at least for a short time. In a 1997 study, Mark Carhart was the first to use momentum, together with the Fama-French market beta, size and value factors, to explain mutual fund returns. Initial research on momentum was published in 1993.

The authors used a bootstrapping technique (rather than a Monte Carlo simulation) to simulate returns in a way that preserved the autocorrelation observed in markets. The bootstrap simulations (random sampling from the actual empirical distribution) resulted in alternative histories for the market and the four factor premiums. They

High-quality companies have the following traits: low earnings volatility, high margins, high asset turnover (indicating the efficient use of assets), low financial leverage, low operating leverage (indicating a strong balance sheet and low macroeconomic risk), and low stock-specific risk (volatility that is unexplained by macroeconomic activity). The quality factor (QMJ) was introduced in a 2013 study.

then used these histories to generate terminal wealth distributions from investing $1 across alternative investment strategies. The alternative investment strategies they considered were an investment in the global equity market, an investment in the global market complemented by an overlay in a risk premium (each factor considered independently), and an investment in the market complemented by an overlay of an equal-weighted (1/N) allocation to each factor premium. In the single-factor cases, the overlay is $1 invested in the long side of the premium and $1 invested in the short side. In the case including all four factors, each factor has $0.25 invested in the long side and $0.25 invested in the short side. The portfolios were rebalanced monthly.

The following table shows the terminal wealth at various percentiles of performance. For example, while $1 invested in the global market grows to a median value of $4.17 after 20 years, the fifth percentile of terminal wealth shows a value of $1.06, the first percentile shows a loss of 44 percent, and the top percentile (the 99th) shows an increase of more than twentyfold.

PERCENTILE	GLOBAL MKT	GLOBAL MKT & SMB	GLOBAL MKT & HML	GLOBAL MKT & UMD	GLOBAL MKT & QMJ	GLOBAL MKT & PREMIA PORTF
0.01	0.56	0.53	1.16	1.19	2.46	1.52
0.05	1.06	1.09	2.27	2.65	3.62	2.68
0.10	1.46	1.52	3.20	4.07	4.44	3.60
0.25	2.46	2.67	5.56	7.96	6.25	5.65
0.50	4.17	4.86	9.97	16.13	8.96	9.10
0.75	7.01	8.62	16.94	32.34	12.56	14.45
0.90	10.56	13.72	26.96	56.30	16.88	20.92
0.95	13.02	18.32	34.68	79.38	19.87	25.93
0.99	20.30	30.85	55.97	147.53	26.76	36.65

SMB (THE SIZE PREMIUM, SMALL MINUS BIG); HML (THE VALUE PREMIUM, HIGH MINUS LOW); UMD (THE MOMENTUM PREMIUM, UP MINUS DOWN); QMJ (THE QUALITY PREMIUM, QUALITY MINUS JUNK)

Note that with the sole exception of the first percentile of the portfolio that includes the global market plus the size factor overlay, the outcomes are improved over just the global market portfolio. That particular outcome is due to the procyclical nature of the size factor. However, results are quite different when we look at the portfolio with the quality factor overlay. This should not be surprising because the quality factor tends to outperform in negative market environments. With that said, the downside protection did not come with an offsetting reduction in terminal wealth at any percentile. In all cases, relative to the global market portfolio, the 1/N diversified portfolio containing all four factors produced dramatically superior results, enhancing both downside protection and terminal wealth in good environments.

WHAT IF FACTOR PREMIUMS DECLINE?

Given that research has shown factor premiums tend, on average, to shrink by about one-third post-publication, Scott and Cavaglia next considered what would happen if the factor premiums shrunk to half their historical levels. As the following table shows, the portfolio of factor premiums continues to mitigate most of the unfortunate tail (the lower 5 percent of cases) in which the investor's terminal wealth is lower than at the starting point while simultaneously improving terminal wealth in almost all other cases. The 1/N overlay portfolio has higher terminal wealth in all percentiles, and avoids a loss even at the first percentile.

PERCENTILE	GLOBAL MKT	GLOBAL MKT & SMB	GLOBAL MKT & HML	GLOBAL MKT & UMD	GLOBAL MKT & QMJ	GLOBAL MKT & PREMIA PORTF
0.01	0.56	0.48	0.75	0.55	1.59	1.00
0.05	1.06	0.97	1.48	1.32	2.40	1.76
0.10	1.46	1.37	2.08	2.01	3.03	2.38
0.25	2.46	2.44	3.60	3.99	4.23	3.78
0.50	4.17	4.41	6.36	8.23	5.99	6.15
0.75	7.01	7.85	11.03	16.19	8.49	9.65
0.90	10.56	12.86	17.53	28.37	11.40	14.11
0.95	13.02	16.86	22.90	38.70	13.55	17.29
0.99	20.30	27.51	36.21	70.31	18.55	24.96

SMB (THE SIZE PREMIUM, SMALL MINUS BIG); HML (THE VALUE PREMIUM, HIGH MINUS LOW); UMD (THE MOMENTUM PREMIUM, UP MINUS DOWN); QMJ (THE QUALITY PREMIUM, QUALITY MINUS JUNK)

Scott and Cavaglia also performed an interesting test. They compared the performance of a portfolio fully invested in global equities and managed by an investor with market-timing skill set at 10 percent (meaning the investor could accurately forecast 10 percent of bear markets, a high hurdle given the lack of evidence supporting the view that bear markets can be forecasted) with the performance of a strategy fully invested in global equities and with an overlay of equally weighted factor premiums. They found that the distribution of terminal wealth across all percentiles is greater for the factor premiums strategy than for the skill-based strategy. In other words, the factor premiums strategy dominates the skill-based one, creating a very high hurdle for active management in terms of the ability to time markets.

DOES FACTOR DIVERSIFICATION MAKE
THE ROAD LESS BUMPY?

In addition, Scott and Cavaglia tested to see if the factor portfolio allowed investors to "sleep better," perhaps improving their ability to stay disciplined and avoid panicked selling. They noted that the median value of the drawdowns for a strategy fully invested in the global market was 0.43 (a loss of 43 percent), suggesting that investors will be exposed to at least one sizable and very nasty event on their journey toward achieving their retirement goals. The authors found that the overlay portfolio can smooth the ride, providing smaller drawdowns at every percentile, even with the 50 percent haircut to the premiums applied.

Scott and Cavaglia also considered the utility of downside protection. The research shows that investors are, on average, risk-averse. Therefore, they are willing to "buy insurance" (that is, to accept lower expected returns) to protect themselves against downside losses. Using utility

48

functions, along with varying degrees of risk aversion, they found that in all cases the value of downside protection offered by the factor overlay portfolio (benchmarked against the global market portfolio's profit and loss) is economically large and significant, emphasizing the factor overlay portfolio's protection against individuals' aversion to losses.

The authors showed that the distribution of terminal wealth of a global market portfolio strategy can be significantly enhanced via an overlay that allocates capital equally across the four premiums they studied. In particular, the factor exposures help mitigate downside risk. Importantly, their simulations demonstrated that, even if the average premiums were halved, their drawdown mitigation properties would still be preserved. Finally, they showed that active asset allocation strategies require significant market-timing skill to outperform a passive factor-premium-based overlay strategy.

In summary, the "secret sauce" that produced more efficient portfolios with less tail risk was the addition of unique sources of risk (factors) that carry premiums whose returns have low to negative correlation with traditional stock and bond portfolios. These same concepts can be applied to alternative investments.

As you will recall from our recurring illustration, when shown the two bell curves representing the distribution of potential returns for Portfolios A and B, investors prefer Portfolio B with its narrower distribution. In other words, they prefer the one with more of the weight of the distribution closer to the mean (the expected return). Adding exposure to the size and value factors while reducing exposure to market beta enabled us to develop a portfolio in which the distribution of returns was more like Portfolio B. But what if you could create a portfolio with an even more favorable distribution of returns? Perhaps one whose distribution of returns looks more like Portfolio C as depicted in the graph on the next page?

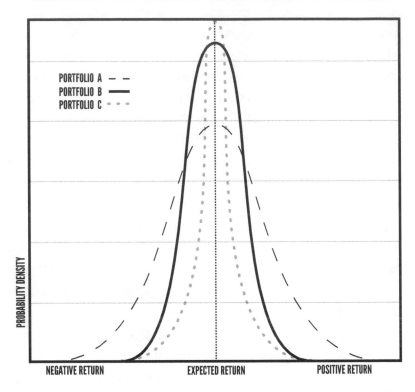

PORTFOLIO A — —
PORTFOLIO B ——
PORTFOLIO C ● ● ●

PROBABILITY DENSITY

NEGATIVE RETURN   EXPECTED RETURN   POSITIVE RETURN

In Part II, we discuss five alternative investments that further shift the potential distribution of returns in a favorable way. The five alternatives are alternative lending, reinsurance, the variance risk premium, AQR Capital Management's Style Premia Alternative Fund and AQR Capital Management's Managed Futures Fund. While the addition of each individual alternative would improve the efficiency of a portfolio, combining them further enhances efficiency because, in each case, the correlation of their returns to each other, as well as to the other assets in the portfolio, is low. The result is like Portfolio C, whose distribution of returns is even more favorable than that of Portfolio B.

PART II

ALTERNATIVE INVESTMENTS

CHAPTER 5:
ALTERNATIVE LENDING

Over the past several years, we have witnessed a fundamental shift in the fixed income landscape. Traditionally, banks have been central to the creation of credit, driven by their ability to take in low-cost deposits and loan out money at higher rates. While non-bank loan channels have always existed parallel to traditional banking, historically these channels were small niches in the overall economy. However, a new breed of lender has emerged to become a significant presence in the market. Initially, they were known as "peer-to-peer lenders" or "marketplace lenders."

The first was Zopa, a U.K.-based platform founded in 2004. Zopa matched consumers who wanted to borrow money directly with individuals who wanted to lend money. It was soon followed by many others, focused across a wide variety of geographies and borrower types. Growth in the space hit an inflection point after the 2008-2009 global financial crisis, driven by a severe contraction in bank lending, an acceleration of online financial services, and an increasing mistrust of, and dislike for, traditional banks.

Today, these technology-based lending platforms, such as Lending Club (consumer loans), Square (small business loans) and SoFi (student loans) are broadly recognized as "alternative lenders." What's more, they are disrupting lending markets and have taken significant market share from traditional banks.

STRUCTURAL COST ADVANTAGE

Because alternative lenders generally are not burdened with the substantial infrastructure costs of traditional banks (they don't have physical branches) or the same level of regulatory oversight (banks are typically regulated by the full spectrum of state bank examiners, the FDIC, the SEC, the Federal Reserve and consumer credit agencies), they are able to extend loans at significantly lower rates. It is also important to note that, while interest rates have fallen dramatically since 2008, the average revolving credit card rate actually has risen. Alternative lenders have been able to leverage their superior operating efficiency to offer more attractive pricing to consumer and small business borrowers while also delivering a seemingly superior service experience.

The increasing cost structure at banks in the post-Dodd-Frank Act era (after 2010) makes it increasingly uneconomic to originate smaller business loans. Even though, following the financial crisis, U.S. banks significantly expanded their portfolio of business loans of over $1 million, at the same time they have pulled away from making smaller loans. With few viable alternatives, many small business owners have resorted to borrowing on credit cards, taking on debt that often has a punitively high, variable rate. For instance, *The Wall Street Journal* reported in November 2015 that, at one of the largest U.S. banks, small-business credit cards accounted for more than 90 percent of lending to businesses with less than $1 million in revenue. As a result, alternative lending platforms have been steadily taking market share by catering to this underserved segment and cost-effectively originating smaller loans.

The biggest impact has been on small banks and, thus, on small businesses, because small banks make the vast majority of small business loans. For example, the number of banks with less than $100 million in assets declined by 85 percent from 1985 to 2013. And the trend continues unabated. Not only do alternative lenders have a cost structure advantage, but, as mentioned previously, their technology enables them to provide arguably better service, including faster turnaround times.

It is important to note the difference between consumer loans, which are often uncollateralized, and small business loans, which typically are secured either by business assets, the business owner personally, or both.

WORLDWIDE PHENOMENON

Alternative lending is not just a U.S. phenomenon. There now are hundreds of alternative lending platforms around the world. In the United States alone, alternative lenders originated an estimated $30 billion in loans in 2016, and are expected to generate $150 billion in loans by 2020. The opportunity is enormous, as those figures remain just a small fraction of the nearly $900 billion in revolving U.S. consumer credits now outstanding. In addition, the market for small business loans in the United States is about $300 billion.

Student loans present another area of opportunity for alternative lenders, with the U.S. market totaling about $1.4 trillion. Student loans historically have been "one-size-fits-all." The result is that high-credit-quality borrowers pay the same rate as low-credit-quality borrowers. Alternative lending platforms can target borrowing students with high credit ratings (thus lowering expected losses from defaults), providing meaningful cost savings.

Furthermore, just as U.S. prime consumer borrowers frequently pay very high rates on revolving credit loans, borrowers in other parts of the developed world also often pay interest of more than 20 percent for bank credit. That has fueled the global expansion of alternative lending in the consumer market.

SOURCES OF DEMAND: CONSUMER LOANS

Though each alternative lending platform has a slightly different niche in the market, consumers often view these loans as an alternative to credit card debt. Credit cards can carry high interest rates, and the average cost of credit card debt has risen in recent years even as interest rates in the broader economy generally have fallen. Consumers who take loans from platforms like Lending Club and SoFi are often attracted to lower interest rates, at least relative to credit cards, as well as their reputation for enhanced customer service. Also, unlike credit card debt, loans originated by alternative lending platforms generally are fixed rate and fully amortizing.

SOURCES OF DEMAND: BUSINESS LOANS

Alternative lenders are filling a gap left by traditional banks as they have, in many cases, pulled away from small businesses term loans. According to the same November 2015 *Wall Street Journal* article, it costs one large U.S. bank roughly the same to originate a $100,000 small business loan as it did for it to originate a loan of $1 million. Small business credit cards cost the bank a lot less to issue. But credit cards are a relatively expensive way for businesses to finance growth. Alternative lenders have figured out how to originate smaller-sized loans to small businesses in an operationally efficient way.

Alternative loans to small business borrowers tend to be about $75,000 to $150,000, and they typically go to companies with revenue in the range of $1 million to $2 million. Common uses for the proceeds include business expansion, inventory, financing property, and plant and equipment purchases.

SOURCE OF CAPITAL FOR ALTERNATIVE LENDERS

The industry overcame two significant early hurdles to get where it is today. The first was that borrowers wanted their money quickly, but the platforms first had to find willing lenders. The matching process was not conducive to good service. The second problem was the information asymmetry between the individual borrower and the individual lender. Specifically, the lender did not know the borrower's credibility as well as the reverse. Such information asymmetry can result in adverse selection. Fortunately, financial intermediaries began to replace individuals as lenders, buying loans from well-known alternative loan originators. Today, institutions are the predominant source of funding for alternative loans. For example, Lending Club, the largest U.S. platform, shifted from 100 percent retail funding in 2008 to 84 percent institutional funding in 2015.

Alternative lenders prefer institutional capital because it makes the loan funding process faster from the borrower's perspective. Institutional buyers typically buy whole loans, whereas it can take weeks for retail investors to fund a loan in fractional increments. And from a strategic perspective, dedicated institutional capital is more stable, allowing the platforms to grow responsibly.

Institutional investors were able to provide funding by creating investment products, such as closed-end "interval" funds, that individual investors can utilize to access the market. These funds are not mutual funds because they do not provide daily liquidity. After all, you need committed capital to make term loans. Instead, they provide for redemptions (with limits) at regular intervals (such as quarterly).

This type of financial intermediary can help reduce asymmetric information risk by setting strong credit standards (such as requiring a high FICO score), performing extensive due diligence on the originators (to make sure their credit culture is strong), structuring repayments in ways that can improve performance (such as requiring that all loans be fully amortizing and that automatic ACH repayments are made on individual loans, thereby eliminating the choice of which loans to pay off, as with credit card debt) and requiring the originator to buy back all loans shown to be fraudulent. They can also require that business loans be repaid directly from sales receipts. Additionally, they can enhance credit quality by utilizing social media to confirm information on the credit application. By improving transparency, they also facilitate the flow of capital to borrowers in a more efficient and dependable manner.

THE IMPORTANCE OF CREDIT QUALITY: THE EVIDENCE

Riza Emekter, Yanbin Tu, Benjamas Jirasakuldech and Min Lu contribute to the literature on alternative lending platforms with the study "Evaluating Credit Risk and Loan Performance in Online Peer-to-Peer (P2P) Lending," which appeared in the January 2015 issue of *Applied Economics*. Their dataset consisted of more than 61,000 loans, totaling more than $700 million, originated by the Lending Club in the period from May 2007 to June 2012. Almost 70 percent of loans requested were related to credit card debt or debt consolidation. The next leading purpose for borrowing was to pay home mortgage debt or to remodel a home. The following is a summary of the authors' findings:

- Borrowers with a high FICO score, high credit grade, low revolving line utilization, low debt-to-income ratio and who own a home are associated with low default risk. This was consistent with a finding from Jefferson Duarte, Stephan Siegel and Lance Young in the study "Trust and Credit: The Role of Appearance in Peer-to-Peer Lending," which appeared in the August 2012 issue of *The Review of Financial Studies*.

- It is important to screen out borrowers with low FICO scores, high revolving line utilization and high debt-to-income ratios, and to attract the highest-FICO-score borrowers, to significantly reduce default risk. The higher interest rate charged for the riskier borrower is not significant enough to justify the higher default probability.

Emekter, Tu, Jirasakuldech and Lu's findings on credit risk are consistent with those of Zhiyong Li, Xiao Yao, Qing Wen and Wei Yang, authors of the March 2016 study "Prepayment and Default of Consumer Loans in Online Lending." They, too, found that default can be accurately predicted by a range of variables. The authors noted that increased prepayment risk exists with consumer loans because the lenders don't charge any early prepayment penalties. However, if the lender requires that all loans be fully amortizing, and none are long-term (typically three- to five-year maturity), duration risk is relatively small. Of course, loans that prepay have eliminated the risk of a later default.

DIVERSIFICATION BENEFITS

In addition to relatively high yields with relatively short durations, investing in alternative loans also provides some diversification benefits. The reason is that their correlation with the equity markets tends to be low, except during periods when unemployment rises dramatically (such as during the global financial crisis of 2008-2009). For example, equity markets experienced significant losses in January 2016. However, there was no concurrent downturn in the economy that would have caused consumer defaults to rise. Investors saw the same thing following the Brexit vote in June 2016. In both cases, while equity markets were falling, the performance of these loans was unaffected. Thus, there are times, though not all times, when an investment in these loans will help to dampen portfolio volatility.

Furthermore, buying a portfolio of consumer loans diversified by geography (by states and even countries) as well as by profession/industry comes with certain benefits. For example, the ability of a dentist in London to pay back a loan versus a retailer in New York is likely to have a low correlation. Even within the United States, states each possess a micro-economy that doesn't necessarily move in tandem with others (for instance, well-publicized oil price declines in 2016 only impacted a few areas). It is important also to understand that consumer credit is somewhat different from corporate credit. There are examples of recessions that affected corporate balance sheets while consumer credit performed relatively well (2001 is a recent example).

There are some other issues, however, that merit consideration.

ASSET LOCATION

Given that all the income from loans purchased from alternative lending platforms will be ordinary and, thus, taxed at the highest rates, investors should prefer to hold this asset in tax-advantaged accounts. Low-tax-bracket investors, however, could consider holding it in taxable accounts. In certain situations, though, it may be appropriate for high-tax-bracket investors to use this asset in taxable accounts as an alternative to municipal bonds. Such investors would accept incremental credit risk in exchange for a higher expected after-tax return and less duration (inflation) risk.

Because interval funds do not provide daily liquidity, they cannot be held inside a 401(k) plan unless the participant has created a self-directed brokerage account.

THE ROLE OF FIXED INCOME

While, on average, the correlation of alternative loans to equity (market beta) risk tends to be low, it is important to understand that the correlation will rise during economic downturns, when unemployment, and thus credit losses, increase. The main role fixed income should play in a portfolio is to dampen its overall risk to an acceptable level. As a result, unless an investor has a very low equity allocation, and also has both the ability and willingness to accept more risk, an allocation to this asset likely should be taken from a portfolio's equity portion.

SUMMARY

Until quite recently, most investors have not had direct access to the consumer, small business and student loan credit risk premium. The alternative lending industry offers that access, as well as benefits to both borrowers (by reducing the high cost of bank credit, credit card debt and payday loans while delivering better service) and to investors (by providing opportunities to earn higher yields).

Today, with the proper controls in place, investing in these alternative loans can offer an attractive complement to a fixed income portfolio. While they do entail incremental credit risk, alternative loans also currently provide sufficiently high yields to permit high forward-looking return expectations (after expected default losses) relative to other alternative investment strategies. At the same time, given that the average duration on a portfolio of alternative loans is only expected to be about 18 months, term risk and related inflation risk is significantly reduced relative to a typical intermediate-term bond portfolio. Thus, there is a trade-off — lower term and inflation risk, but more credit risk. That trade-off is made more favorable by the presence of a significant premium for both credit risk and illiquidity.

Our recommendation that alternative lending assets are worthy of consideration may seem contrary to our longstanding position that investors should limit fixed income to only the safest vehicles (such as Treasuries, government agencies, FDIC-insured CDs and AAA/AA-rated municipals that are also general obligation or essential service revenue bonds). The reason for our original recommendation was that research has shown corporate credit risk has not been well rewarded, especially after considering fund expenses. In this case, however, while alternative lending assets are not of the same quality as the aforementioned safe bonds, the evidence shows that investors have been well rewarded. It is just that, until recently, the general public has had no access to these investments. They instead resided on the balance sheets of banks and other lenders. Fintech firms have disrupted that model and investment management firms have now provided access to investors.

RISK AND EXPECTED RETURNS

The term "expected return" or "forward-looking return expectation" is a statistical estimation for the compound return of an asset class over the long term. It is important to understand that expected returns are the mean of a very wide potential distribution of possible returns. Thus, they are not a guarantee of future results. Expected returns are forward-looking forecasts, and are subject to numerous assumptions, risks and uncertainties, which change over time. Actual results may differ materially from those anticipated in an expected-return forecast. With those caveats in mind, our estimate for the expected return to prime alternative loans is similar to what we expect for the U.S. stock market, though with only about one-quarter of the volatility — an attractive combination.

ACCESSING ALTERNATIVE LOANS

Historically, consumer and small business credit risk underwritten by banks was not shared directly with outside investors. Fortunately, we can now directly access these attractive assets through interval funds, such as the Stone Ridge Alternative Lending Risk Premium Interval Fund (LENDX), the RiverNorth Marketplace Lending Fund (RMPLX) and the Colchis P2P Income Fund (a limited partnership). Our preferred vehicle, the one we recommend for our clients, is LENDX.

CHAPTER 6:
REINSURANCE

While nobody "likes" to buy insurance, every year consumers spend trillions of dollars on insurance policies. We do not, however, buy insurance to protect ourselves against regular, predictable events. Rather, we budget for such expenses. On the other hand, when dealing with the possibility of rare, unpredictable downside events — such as premature death, disability or destruction of property from a fire, earthquake or hurricane — we do buy insurance to protect ourselves against an outcome too risky to bear on our own. The premiums we pay transfer risk, with buyers seeking to eliminate the effects of an extreme, negative event.

The price that the insurance company charges to bear the risk of extreme events, which can lead to large losses, decomposes into two parts: an expected payout and a risk premium to compensate the seller for the uncertain nature of any payout, which may be sudden and dramatic. In other words, when individuals buy insurance, they hope, and expect, to incur a loss (they anticipate that, on average, the insurance company will generate a profit).

REINSURANCE

Reinsurers are an important part of the overall insurance industry. But, while most people are familiar with at least a few of the largest insurance companies, reinsurers generally are not household names because they do not deal directly with consumers.

Reinsurance is insurance that is purchased by an insurance company as a means of risk management, allowing them both to service their clients (selling more insurance than they have capital to otherwise support) and to diversify risks. The reinsurer is paid a reinsurance premium by the "ceding company," which issues insurance policies to its own policyholders.

Many traditional reinsurers have legacies reaching back to the mid-1800s. Typically highly diversified, reinsurers offer protection on a broad spectrum of client risks. That broad diversification across uncorrelated risks is what allows reinsurers to be "structurally levered." Regulators allow reinsurers to hold substantially less capital than their total exposure because it is highly unlikely that losses will occur simultaneously across uncorrelated and geographically dispersed risks. As an example, a reinsurance company whose risks are highly diversified might be required to hold $2 of capital for every $5 of reinsurance risk.

Collectively, the reinsurance industry had about $600 billion of capital in 2017. Since the 1990s, Insurance-Linked Securities (ILSs) have allowed investors to participate directly in reinsurance risks.

INVESTMENT OPPORTUNITY

The reinsurance industry's existence presents an opportunity for investors to add an asset, through participation in the reinsurance business, with equity-like expected returns uncorrelated with the risks and returns of other assets in their portfolios (stocks, bonds and other alternative investments). Stock market crashes don't cause earthquakes, hurricanes or other natural disasters. The reverse is also generally true — natural disasters tend not to cause bear markets in stocks or bonds. This lack of correlation, combined with equity-like returns, results in a more efficient portfolio, specifically one with a higher Sharpe ratio (meaning it has a higher return for each unit of risk).

Historically, insurers and reinsurers' capital base consisted of traditional debt and equity. However, since Hurricane Andrew in 1992, and especially since the tumultuous hurricane season of 2005, the industry increasingly has turned to third-party capital. The interaction between the reinsurance markets and the capital markets is known as "convergence." Through convergence, investors are able to participate directly in the catastrophe risk space, rather than being forced to simply buy the debt or equity of insurance and reinsurance companies. Today, about 12 percent of the capital committed to reinsurance comes from third-party investors, not reinsurers themselves.

DIVERSIFICATION BENEFIT

Consider that there is no logical reason to believe losses from earthquakes should be correlated with returns to stocks, bonds, commodities or currencies, or any factor in which you can invest (such as momentum or the carry trade). In addition, a well-run reinsurance fund should be diversified across types of events whose losses are also uncorrelated. For example, a well-diversified reinsurance fund might invest in policies covering losses from fire, tornados, earthquakes, hurricanes, political risks, harm to fine art and damage while goods are in transport (marine and on land). Again, each of these risks generally should be uncorrelated — there is no basis to think that losses from earthquakes correlate with losses from hurricanes.

What's more, today we are seeing innovative new insurance products that protect against losses from hacking, business interruption, concert cancellations and even insufficient snow at ski resorts. Such offerings present further diversification opportunities.

THE IMPORTANCE OF GLOBAL DIVERSIFICATION

Reinsurers also should diversify each of their risks globally because, for example, the risk of earthquakes in the United States is uncorrelated to the risk of earthquakes elsewhere around the world. The last earthquake that caused major losses in California had a magnitude of 6.9 on the Richter scale. It occurred in October 1989. The last major quake in Turkey was a 7.6 magnitude event that occurred in August 1999; the last major quake in China was a 7.9 magnitude event that occurred in May 2008; the last major quake in Japan was a 9.0 magnitude event that occurred in March 2011; and, in 2016, central Italy experienced a series of significant earthquakes beginning in August and continuing into October, with the largest being a 6.6 magnitude event. While it is certainly possible multiple major earthquakes can occur in the same year, it is not that likely. Additionally, because other types of risk that reinsurance usually covers are uncorrelated to earthquakes, the risk of a catastrophic portfolio loss is greatly reduced. In technical terms, the negative skewness of a diversified reinsurance program is much less than it is for any one type of insurance risk.

It is important to understand that the equity-like expected returns associated with accepting the risks of an investment in reinsurance are compensation for the chance of occasional large losses. As with equities, writing insurance against extreme, but rare, events comes with accepting negative skewness in the distribution of returns. Because investors dislike negative skewness, they demand a large premium for accepting such risks (resulting in a high expected, but not guaranteed, return). And as noted, a well-structured reinsurance fund can minimize the risk of negative skewness by diversifying across many different types of risk and across the globe.

A reinsurance strategy, like all risky investments, does have the potential to incur significant losses. But, when those losses occur, insurers and reinsurers raise premiums to restore their capital. Thus, the highest expected return to insurers and reinsurers tends to be after catastrophic losses. Patience and disciplined rebalancing are keys to successfully harvesting the reinsurance premium over time.

The bottom line is that reinsurance risks help diversify the risks of a traditional stock and fixed income portfolio while also offering potentially higher returns. In addition, reinsurance offers the potential for equity-like returns with less volatility (about half) and less downside risk than equities. Furthermore, the returns to reinsurance are uncorrelated to the returns of all the other assets in a typical portfolio. We believe the most effective method for gaining exposure to the reinsurance premium is to invest in a fund that partners with large reinsurance firms through the purchase of quota shares, eliminating the market beta risk investors would incur if they instead owned reinsurance company stocks. Indeed, market beta risk would account for roughly 80 percent of the total risk of a reinsurance company's stock. In other words, we want to isolate and hold only the risk specific to reinsurance. We also want to minimize the concentration risk associated with catastrophe bonds (which tend to have the vast majority of their risk profile connected to losses from hurricanes in the United States), another element of investing in reinsurance.

QUOTA SHARES

In a quota share arrangement, a fund receives a specified percentage of the premium of a defined book of reinsurance business (say, 5 percent of a reinsurer's global natural catastrophe business) and also pays the same percentage of the losses (5 percent in our example). Quota shares, which transfer risk from the reinsurance company to the fund, are typically one-year agreements. Thus, just as was the case with alternative lending, fund families generally use closed-end interval funds because they avoid the daily liquidity requirements of open-ended mutual funds.

Reinsurance companies incur high costs in originating business (underwriters, risk models, office overhead, etc.). However, the marginal cost of origination is less than the average cost. The investing fund typically agrees to share in the expenses at a rate attractive to both sides. Additionally, the ceding company usually agrees to cap the interval fund's maximum loss at the amount of collateral posted. The interval fund puts up the required capital as collateral to demonstrate that it has the capacity to pay claims.

The extra capacity gained by ceding premiums to the interval fund allows reinsurers to underwrite more protection for their insurance company clients without straining their capital. In return, investors get access to an aligned, diversified pool of risk that has equity-like expected returns. Quota shares permit access to broader classes of reinsurance risk and offer an opportunity for higher returns (but with less liquidity) than catastrophe bonds, to which the fund also typically will have some limited exposure. The added diversification benefit is one reason we prefer funds that use quota share arrangements to access the reinsurance premium.

CATASTROPHE BONDS

Catastrophe (cat) bonds are risk-linked, high-yielding, non-investment-grade debt instruments that transfer a specified set of risks from the issuer to investors. Most typically, they are linked to losses from hurricanes in the United States. As of 2017, the cat bond market had grown to about $25 billion since the first issuance in 1994. Cat bonds are mainly used to provide liquidity for the reinsurance fund. Of course, these bonds are inherently risky and usually have maturities of less than three years. If no catastrophe occurs, the insurance company pays a coupon to investors. However, if a catastrophe does occur, the principal would be forgiven and the insurance company would use this money to pay their claimholders. The natural attraction of cat bonds is that there is no reason to believe events such as natural disasters are correlated with the risks of other financial assets.

Thus, cat bonds offer a source of potential return truly unrelated to other major asset classes (drops in the S&P 500 Index or actions by the Federal Reserve don't cause earthquakes and hurricanes). And, in general, the reverse is also true. As a result, they provide diversification benefits.

Steven Clark, Mike Dickson Jr. and Faith Roberts Neale contribute to the literature on cat bonds with their July 2016 study "Portfolio Diversification Effects of Catastrophe Bonds," which covers the 14-year period from 2002 through 2015. The authors observe that from January 2006 to December 2014, the Eurekahedge ILS Advisers Index showed negative returns in only seven out of 108 months. The largest negative monthly return, -3.94 percent, was in March 2011, the month the Tohoku earthquake occurred. The second largest monthly loss was just -0.74 percent, in September 2008, followed by the third largest loss, -0.57 percent, in October 2008.

To test their diversification benefit hypothesis, Clark, Dickson and Neale analyzed cat bonds in several different ways. The following is a summary of their findings:

- Because their correlations with other financial assets are low, strong support exists for the notion that cat bonds provide substantial diversification benefits when they are added to an investment opportunity set already consisting of traditional asset classes (U.S. equities, international equities, bonds, commodities and real estate).

- Cat bonds demonstrate significant portfolio diversification benefits in various out-of-sample analyses, including naïve 1/N strategies (where N is the number of factors, asset classes or investments being considered) and when using a mean-variance model, a minimum-variance model and a volatility-timing model.

- The payoffs from cat bonds cannot be replicated in the mean-variance space by portfolios holding only other asset classes.

- The standard deviation of cat bonds is much smaller than the standard deviations shown by other indices, contributing to a significantly greater Sharpe ratio (which assumes normal distributions). However, the cat bond index does display extreme kurtosis and has the longest left tail (you would expect large losses when low-probability, but high-risk, events occur).

- Cat bonds added substantial diversification benefits during the 2008 global financial crisis, reducing drawdown measures and conditional value-at-risk in times of market distress.

Cat bonds' diversification benefits were confirmed by Peter Carayannopoulos and M. Fabricio Perez, authors of the 2015 study "Diversification through Catastrophe Bonds: Lessons from the Subprime Financial Crisis." However, they also found that cat bonds were not zero-market-beta assets during the 2008 financial crisis. In fact, the dynamic correlation coefficients of cat bonds with the market and the corresponding hedge ratios were statistically and significantly positive during the crisis. They believe that the rising correlation between cat bonds and the market was caused by the "structure of CAT bond trust accounts and the composition of the assets used as collateral in the trust account."

The authors go on to add: "Assets used as collateral in these trust accounts proved to be of lesser than expected quality and, furthermore, counterparties in swap agreements, put in place in an effort to immunise collateral asset returns from market fluctuations, were exposed to considerable credit risk or even defaulted during the crisis."

The good news is that Carayannopoulos and Perez found the effects of the financial crisis on cat bonds had disappeared by 2011, as their correlation with the market returned to its statistically insignificant, pre-crisis levels. They noted: "These results may imply that the new and improved collateral structures created for CAT bonds issued after 2009 have been perceived as effective by market participants. These new structures attempt to enhance the credit quality of the collateral asset and include limits to the type of assets permitted in the collateral account, and constant monitoring and reporting of the collateral account balance."

Despite their lack of an investment-grade rating, cat bonds typically do not entail credit risk because they are fully collateralized with proceeds, generally in U.S. Treasury money market products. They also are generally floating-rate notes, with minimal duration risk. In terms of performance, while 2018's bond yields tend to be lower than in the not-so-distant past, for the period from January 2002 through June 2016, the Swiss Re CAT Bond Index returned 8.0 percent versus 7.4 percent for high-yield bonds and 6.4 percent for the S&P 500 Index.

While past performance is no guarantee of future results, during this time period cat bonds not only produced better returns than high-yield bonds or the S&P 500 Index, but they did so with the lowest volatility (2.4 percent versus 6.6 percent for high-yield bonds and 17.3 percent for the S&P 500 Index). They also experienced a smaller maximum drawdown, just 4.3 percent versus 26.5 percent for high-yield bonds and 55.3 percent for the S&P 500 Index.

In short, cat bonds provide liquidity and diversification for a well-diversified interval fund whose risks consist mostly of quota shares.

RISK AND EXPECTED RETURN

As we have discussed, expected return is a statistical estimation for the compound return of an asset class over the long term. It is important to understand that expected returns are the mean of a very wide potential distribution of possible returns. Thus, they are not a guarantee of future results. Expected returns are forward-looking forecasts, and are subject to numerous assumptions, risks and uncertainties, which change over time. Actual results may differ materially from those anticipated in an expected return forecast.

Again with these caveats in mind, our expected return estimate for a well-diversified, quota shares-based fund is similar to the expected return for U.S. equities. Our estimate for a best-case year (meaning losses from catastrophic events are less than expected) is a return of about 11 percent to 12 percent. Investors should also expect that, in about 10 percent of years, losses will be about 10 percent. In a year like 2005, when three major hurricanes, including Hurricane Katrina, hit the United States, losses in such a fund would likely be in the 15 percent to 20 percent range. 2017, which also had three major hurricanes as well as two major wildfires in California, saw losses in the low double digits. Reinsurance losses larger than any ever experienced historically might cause a fund to lose somewhere in the range of 30 percent to 40 percent. Keep in mind that when losses occur, premiums are raised to restore capital and incorporate the new risk information.

ASSET LOCATION

Because a reinsurance strategy is tax inefficient (the income from it is ordinary), investors should strongly prefer to hold this investment in tax-advantaged accounts, unless they are in a low tax bracket. In certain situations, it may be appropriate for high-tax-bracket investors to use a reinsurance strategy in taxable accounts, particularly if it is being employed instead of municipal bonds.

Again, because interval funds do not provide daily liquidity, they cannot be held inside a 401(k) plan unless the participant has created a self-directed brokerage account.

ACCESSING REINSURANCE RISK

There are currently two options investors can utilize to access reinsurance risk: the Stone Ridge Reinsurance Risk Premium Interval Fund (SRRIX) and the Pioneer ILS Interval Fund (XILSX). Our preferred vehicle, the one we recommend for our clients, is SRRIX.

The next three chapters, which cover the variance risk premium, the alternative style premium and time-series momentum, examine more complex strategies that, to many, may not be as intuitive as alternative lending and reinsurance strategies. We have done our best to provide clear explanations.

CHAPTER 7:
THE VARIANCE RISK PREMIUM

Economists have long puzzled over the simultaneous demand from consumers for risk-reducing insurance and risk-increasing lottery tickets. Every year, people spend trillions of dollars on the two combined. These behaviors may seem unrelated, but they actually are symmetrical forms of risk transfer. The insurance policy is a means of risk transfer in which a buyer pays to eliminate the possibility of an extreme, rare, downside event — such as premature death, destruction from an earthquake or hurricane, or an equity market crash — while the lottery ticket is a means of risk transfer in which a buyer pays to create the possibility of an extreme, rare, upside event.

Again, the price of such a risk transfer decomposes into two parts: an expected payout and a risk premium to compensate the seller for the uncertain nature of any payout, which may be sudden and dramatic. Financial markets are full of strategies that resemble insurance or lotteries. For example, in options markets, the premium to compensate the seller for the uncertain nature of the payout is called the variance (or volatility) risk premium (VRP). This risk premium is rational for both the buyer and the seller. The buyer willingly pays it to create, or to eliminate, uncertainty.

The seller charges it for taking the risk. The evidence indicates that the more remote the risk, the higher the ratio of risk premium to expected payout. Over a large sample size, an expected fair value is set by the probabilities of outcomes, and options sellers charge a premium to that fair value in compensation for providing a risk-transfer service.

The VRP refers to the fact that, over time, the option-implied volatility has tended to exceed the realized volatility of the same underlying asset. This has created a profit opportunity for volatility sellers — those willing to write volatility insurance options, collect the premiums and bear the risk that realized volatility will increase by more than implied volatility. Investors are willing to pay a premium because risky assets, such as stocks, tend to perform poorly when volatility increases. In other words, markets tend to crash down, not up. Thus, the VRP isn't an anomaly we should expect to be arbitraged away. Because the VRP's risks (specifically, the sale of options performs poorly) tend to show up in bad times (when risky assets perform poorly), we should expect a significant premium. Another way to think about this is that investors pay to hedge catastrophic outcomes; they want to transfer the risk of a terrible outcome, like their house burning down or the price of oil going to $200 per barrel. Thus, they knowingly and willingly pay above fair value to eliminate that risk. As a result, the VRP should be considered a unique risk premium that individuals with long investment horizons and stable finances can harvest because they have the ability to accept cyclical risks that show up in bad times.

HISTORICAL EVIDENCE

Data going back as far as 1873 shows the existence of a VRP. In the paper "Option Markets and Implied Volatility: Past Versus Present," published in the November 2009 issue of *The Journal of Financial Economics*, Scott Mixon presented the results from his analysis of data hand-collected from newspapers published between 1873 and 1875. Mixon calculated implied and subsequently realized volatility, and found that options prices reflected a persistent, large and positive spread of 11.8 percentage points between implied and realized volatility for the most liquid options. That is a huge risk premium. Today, markets are more liquid, more transparent and more efficient. Thus, we should not expect to see such a large premium.

Graham Rennison and Niels Pedersen, authors of the September 2012 paper "The Volatility Risk Premium," studied the period from June 1994 through June 2012 and 14 volatility markets, including markets associated with stocks, bonds, commodities and currencies. They found strong evidence of a variance risk premium, with its magnitude ranging from 0.9 percent in currencies to 2.2 percent in equity indices, 2.9 percent in 10-year interest rate swaptions and 4.4 percent in commodities futures. They concluded that the risk-return trade-off in volatility strategies compares favorably to traditional stock and bond strategies, and that these strategies exhibit low correlation to equities. They also found that Sharpe ratios ranged from 0.7 for currencies to 1.2 for U.S. interest rates and commodity futures. These compare favorably to the historical 0.4 Sharpe ratio for the market beta premium. Thus, the authors recommended that investors consider an allocation to VRP strategies.

Using equity index options, Roni Israelov, Lars Nielsen and Daniel Villalon, authors of the study "Embracing Downside Risk," which appears in the Winter 2017 issue of *The Journal of Alternative Investments*, showed that the vast majority of the equity risk premium derives from accepting downside risk versus seeking participation in the upside. They found that, over the period from 1986 through 2014, greater than 80 percent of the equity risk premium was explained by the willingness to accept downside risk. They also discovered that the ex-post VRP was positive 88 percent of the time and averaged 3.4 percent per year.

Israelov, Nielsen and Villalon found a similar result when they examined the upside and downside risk premium in Treasury bonds, with 62 percent of the excess return coming from the downside. The lower percentage they found in bonds should not be surprising because Treasuries have less downside risk than stocks. When they examined gold, the authors found 100 percent of the excess return was from downside risk. They also found strong results when they looked at credit default swaps, with the return for accepting downside risk accounting for more than 100 percent of the excess return.

In addition, Stone Ridge examined the VRP for the 10 largest stocks over the period from 1996 through 2012, breaking down that period into three sub-periods. The firm's researchers found a persistent and stable premium. From 1996 through 1999, the VRP was 4.3 percent. From 2000 through 2009, the premium was 3.9 percent. And from 2010 through 2012, it was 4.1 percent. Stone Ridge also found strikingly similar patterns in implied volatility curves around the world. In international markets, as in the United States, more short-dated and more out-of-the-money options have higher expected VRP returns in both single-stock and index options.

The VRP has been well documented, and is best known in U.S. equities. For example, the implied volatility of S&P 500 Index options exceeded the realized index volatility 85 percent of the time from January 1990 to September 2014. What's more, options historically have traded at about 4.4 percentage points above subsequent realized volatility. It is important to understand that this should not be interpreted to mean the options market tends to overestimate future volatility. Instead, the more likely explanation is that options prices incorporate a risk, or insurance, premium. Most investors are risk-averse, and so they are willing to pay a premium to hedge downside risk. Buying volatility insurance options provides that hedge or insurance. The large premium also exists because of an imbalance in supply and demand. This imbalance arises because there are likely far more natural buyers of volatility insurance options than there are sellers.

FURTHER EVIDENCE

In his paper "Do Financial Markets Reward Buying or Selling Insurance and Lottery Tickets?", which appeared in the September 2012 issue of the CFA Institute's *Financial Analysts Journal*, Antti Ilmanen found that:

- Selling volatility on either the left tail (insurance) or the right tail (lottery tickets) adds value in the long run.

- As with holding high-volatility, lottery-like investments, buying options-based tail risk insurance against asymmetric payoffs earns poor long-term results.

- The evidence is not restricted to options trading. Carry-seeking and other strategies with asymmetric payoffs are closely related to volatility-selling — all are variants of selling tail risk insurance and have earned positive long-run returns. Furthermore, they often have produced Sharpe ratios higher than that of the equity risk premium.

- Speculative, lottery-like investments have delivered lower risk-adjusted returns than their defensive peers in all major asset classes. The more speculative the strategy, the worse the risk-to-reward ratio becomes.

- The use of leverage in low-volatility strategies appears to boost long-run returns.

Ilmanen concluded: "To interpret the long-run gains from selling financial catastrophe insurance as rational risk premiums seems natural. In contrast, the gains from lottery selling seem better explained by investor irrationality or by such nonstandard preferences as lottery seeking or leverage aversion." He noted that the demand for left tail insurance "focuses on portfolio-level downside protection and is guided by covariance with market and other systematic factors. On the right tail, lottery seeking is best served by more idiosyncratic investments and is guided by asset characteristics."

William Fallon, James Park and Danny Yu contribute to the literature on the VRP with their study "Asset Allocation Implications of the Global Volatility Premium," which appears in the September/October 2015 issue of the CFA Institute's *Financial Analysts Journal*. The purpose of their study was "to provide a comprehensive statistical and economic analysis of the global volatility risk premium, with a special emphasis on its practical role as an institutional holding."

The authors developed a grand volatility composite portfolio (GVCP), which was derived from a dynamic trading strategy applied to a variety of instruments, mainly derivatives. Their dataset consisted of nearly two decades of volatility marks gathered through an assortment of options exchanges and investment dealers. Their research accounts for transaction costs, which have a material impact on performance.

The GVCP is an equal-risk-weighted blend of returns on 34 volatility-sensitive instruments in markets across four asset classes: equities (covering 11 markets that make up almost 90 percent of the MSCI World Index), bonds (covering four 10-year interest rate swaps, denominated in U.S. dollars, euros, sterling and yen, that make up approximately 95 percent of the J.P. Morgan GBI Global Index), currencies (covering nine major currencies, traded against the U.S. dollar, that make up more than three-quarters of non-U.S. global GDP) and commodities (10 contracts covering four major commodity sectors — industrial metals, precious metals, energy and agricultural products — that make up more than half of the S&P GSCI). The authors based their volatility returns primarily on two instruments: variance swaps and options. Their data series has an earliest start date of 1995, with other starting dates varying depending on data availability.

To create series that were comparable across both assets and time, the authors scaled each of the 34 volatility return series to target an annualized volatility of 1 percent each month at trade inception. The scaling was ex-ante, using historical realized volatility calculated monthly with an expanding window and a minimum of 36 observations. To facilitate comparison across asset classes, they then combined the scaled volatility return series on an equal-weighted basis by asset within each asset class. They chose an equal-weighting scheme because of its simplicity and transparency. This approach resulted in four composite volatility return series — for equities, fixed income, currencies and commodities — each of which they then scaled to target 1 percent risk on an ex-ante basis using the methodology described previously. Finally, to facilitate the statistical and economic evaluation of volatility as an asset class, Fallon, Park and Yu combined the four asset class return composites on an equal-weighted basis into a single composite scaled to target 1 percent annualized risk, again using the methodology previously outlined. They called this series the GVCP. The following is a summary of their findings:

- Negative (short) volatility premiums are widespread, statistically significant and economically meaningful. A consistently positive mean for the spread between implied and realized volatility existed in all asset classes and components.

- Selling volatility is profitable in virtually all markets nearly all the time, including the five-year period surrounding September 2008, with a consistently positive mean for volatility returns (but with fat left tails).

- Adding the GVCP in small amounts to typical institutional portfolios would have substantially enhanced long-term returns (increasing the combined Sharpe ratio by as much as 12 percent in the authors' sample) but at the cost of increased short-term tail risk.

- The means of all 34 volatility return series were positive. The annual mean return to the 11 stock components ranged from 2.8 percent to 4.5 percent, and the annual standard deviation ranged from 5.4 percent to 7.9 percent. For the four bond components, the annual mean return ranged from 1.8 percent to 4.0 percent, and the annual standard deviation ranged from 4.6 percent to 14.1 percent. For the nine currencies, the annual mean return ranged from 0.6 percent to 1.3 percent, with the annual standard deviation ranging from 2.1 percent to 4.5 percent. For the 10 commodities, the annual mean return ranged from 0.7 percent to 3.5 percent, with the annual standard deviation ranging from 3.4 percent to 13.4 percent.

With all 34 means positive, and with 32 of them significant at the 1 percent level of confidence and two at the 10 percent level, Fallon, Park and Yu concluded: "This consistency suggests a reliable risk premium whose basis is the persistent excess of implied over realized volatility."

They also concluded: "Equally consistent are the patterns in higher moments, with skewness values often large and negative and excess kurtosis figures large and positive. Taken together, these results indicate that buyers offer insurance-like economic rents to sellers, who earn a steady monthly income in exchange for bearing 'crash' risk — the possibility of severe but empirically infrequent losses." In other words, there is a trade-off between average returns and tail risk, with the worst cases coming in at more than double the magnitude of the best-case positive observations.

It is important to note Fallon, Park and Yu found that, on average, "transaction costs reduce gross returns by 47%, a significant reduction." Thus, patient trading is critical to successfully implement the strategy because investors should want to be a seller, not a buyer, of liquidity. That means accepting tracking-error risk.

The authors also observed that the correlations between the GVCP and each of their volatility return series indicate the possibility for diversification benefits across asset classes — pooling enhances the risk and reward trade-off. Correlations are higher in equities and currencies (composite correlations of 0.88 and 0.83) and lower in fixed income and commodities (composite correlations of 0.54 and 0.69). They found that the Sharpe ratio of the GVCP, which pools by asset class and is the broadest composite, remains more than 31 percent higher than the average Sharpe ratio of the composites (1.02 versus 0.78) and 94 percent higher than the average Sharpe ratio across assets (1.02 versus 0.53). However, they found no improvement in tail risk. In fact, they determined that tail risk events in their sample were "more highly correlated than typical month-to-month returns."

Fallon, Park and Yu concluded that what the GVCP offers is largely distinct from standard explanatory factors (market beta, size and value). The authors write: "Therefore, it may offer unique and additive diversification benefits to traditional portfolios."

THE PERFORMANCE OF THE VRP IN CALM MARKETS

In an earlier study on the VRP, "Still Not Cheap: Portfolio Protection in Calm Markets," which appeared in the Summer 2015 issue of *The Journal of Portfolio Management*, Israelov and Nielsen investigated whether equity portfolio insurance was, historically, a good purchase when the cost of that insurance was relatively cheap — the flip side of selling volatility insurance (earning the VRP). The premise, or theory, behind buying volatility insurance when the cost is relatively cheap is as follows:

- Historically, volatility is mean-reverting.

- Buying put options provides long volatility exposure.

- Go long volatility when it is at historically low levels because volatility is likely to revert to the mean.

Presented in this light, buying put options in calm markets might appear to be a compelling strategy. But does hard data actually support the theory? Israelov and Nielsen begin by noting: "It is well-known that portfolio insurance is expensive on average." Translation: Being *persistently* long volatility is a bad and expensive strategy, and there are more efficient ways to reduce tail risk than buying insurance. For example, for the period from March 15, 2006, through June 20, 2014, Israelov and Nielsen found that buying 5 percent out-of-the-money S&P 500 puts lowered returns by 2.5 percentage points (from 5.2 percent to 2.7 percent) and reduced the Sharpe ratio from 0.37 to 0.21, a decrease of more than 40 percent. The authors also showed that a standalone strategy of buying 5 percent out-of-the-money S&P 500 puts provided an excess return of -2.0 percent per year, and the strategy produced a Sharpe ratio of -0.83. However, such insurance lowered downside market beta considerably, from 0.85 to 0.47. Simply lowering equity exposure would have been a more efficient alternative. But we have yet to answer our question about the VRP in calm markets.

Regarding whether it makes sense to take a tactical approach to volatility (only going long, or to avoid selling when the insurance is cheap), Israelov and Nielsen provided this important insight: "It doesn't matter if implied volatility is at or near its historical low. It doesn't matter if realized volatility is expected to increase. It doesn't even matter if realized volatility actually does increase over the option's life. What does matter is the option's purchase price (implied volatility) relative to its fundamental value (ex-post realized volatility)."

They found that, over the full period for which VIX data was available (from January 2, 1990, through June 30, 2014), the ex-post realized risk premium was 3.4 percent. What's more, it was positive 88 percent of the time. The authors concluded: "Investors who heed analysts' recommendation to purchase options are not only long volatility — they also face long odds of benefiting from the option purchase."

Having determined that being long volatility all the time is a bad strategy, the authors then sought to discover whether it is a good strategy to be long volatility when volatility is low and options prices are historically cheap. Israelov and Nielsen found not only that the realized ex-post variance risk premium was positive in every decile of volatility, but also that the realized premium in the three lowest-volatility buckets, at 3.1 percent, is not much different from the 3.4 percent average from all buckets. Even in the lowest VIX decile, the realized premium was 2.5 percent. They write: "Option prices may be lower, but they remain expensive in the sense that the long volatility component of one-month options is expected to have negative returns."

Upon examining the data, Israelov and Nielsen presented some additional interesting findings. For example: "The volatility risk premium is more variable when implied volatility is high. Its 80% confidence interval is 5% wide in the lowest implied volatility decile and 19% wide in the highest decile. In the lowest risk environment, the most extreme outcome had realized volatility 8% higher than implied volatility. In the highest risk environment, the most extreme outcome occurred when realized volatility was 49% higher than implied volatility. Although owning a put option provides the same contractual protection in each decile per se, the distribution of outcomes across volatility environments has been very different."

In other words, while a 5 percent out-of-the-money put provides the same protection at all times, historically investors have needed the insurance most when volatility is high, not low. The authors concluded that, while the ex-post cost of insurance was lower during times when volatility remained in the lowest three deciles, "less expensive options in calm markets do not necessarily mean that investors are getting a good deal."

They also noted that the maximum 21-day return from the lowest four deciles of volatility was only 1.7 percent. Given that the cost of the options used in their test was more than 1 percent per year, the authors reason that buying them "hardly seems like money well spent."

To examine the robustness of their findings, Israelov and Nielsen also tested whether their results held over a larger universe of equity indices. Specifically, they analyzed index options on the DAX (Germany), Euro Stoxx 50, FTSE (U.K.), Hang Seng (Hong Kong), KOSPI (Korea), NASDAQ, Nikkei (Japan), Russell 2000 and Swiss Market. Internationally, the evidence was very similar to what they found in the United States. For example, from the lowest to the highest volatility quintile, the realized risk premium persistently increased from 1.6 percent to 3.8 percent. They also found similar Sharpe ratios, of about -0.9, across quintiles, with the exception of the highest quintile, where it was much worse at -1.4.

The takeaway is that buying insurance (put options) when volatility is low (the cost is "cheap") is only a good strategy if investors compare it to buying insurance when volatility is high (the cost is expensive).

As a final test, the authors examined the effectiveness of buying insurance against the risk of black swans. They concluded that black swans would need to occur with much greater frequency than they have in the past to make buying insurance an effective strategy. Israelov and Nielsen write: "If you believe that the type of black swan event ... is significantly under-represented in our historical record and you are also willing to pay out more than 1% of NAV per year in order to buy protection for such an event, then purchasing put options may be rationalized." They added this caution: "While it is certainly possible that black swans are under-represented and put options are less expensive than they appear (or even cheaply priced!), we should similarly be willing to also entertain the possibility that black swan events are over-represented in our sample … and put options are even more expensive than they appear."

The research presented by Israelov and Nielsen demonstrates that "put options' low prices during calm periods give the illusion of value." The authors close with this warning: "Buying an option is not a bet that realized volatility will increase; it is a bet that realized volatility will increase above the option's implied volatility. Buying an option is expected to lose money even when volatility is low and rising if the spread between realized and implied volatility is sufficiently high." Said another way, the winning strategy is to be a consistent seller of volatility insurance.

SUMMARY

Diversification has been called the only free lunch in investing. And diversification is investors' only relief from systemic and unforecastable market risks. Effective diversification requires uncorrelated investments, as well as a look beyond traditional stock and bond indices to other areas of risk and return, such as reinsurance, alternative lending and the VRP. Thus, a key to successful investing is pursuing a combination of strategies across low-correlating assets to produce a broadly diversified portfolio.

While the VRP is best known in U.S. equities, and so most volatility products focus on them, diversification across many asset classes has the potential to improve VRP returns through reducing portfolio volatility. This is both intuitive and empirically observable in historical data, which shows low correlations of the VRP across asset classes, including commodities, currencies and credit.

Before investing in the VRP, or any strategy exhibiting negative skewness, you should be aware that, while such strategies can consistently accrue small and regular gains over many years, rare, large losses disproportionately occur in bad times. It is this poor timing of losses that helps explain the large required risk premiums. For example, a simple strategy that involves capturing S&P 500 volatility premium lost more than 48 percent in October 2008. However, volatility premium strategies tend to recover quickly, more so than other asset classes, because it is precisely in the immediate aftermath of a crisis event when the volatility premium is richest. This is similar to how insurance companies, which raise premiums after incurring large losses from catastrophic events, operate.

The potential for large losses means that attempting to monetize the variance risk premium may not be suitable for all investors. However, investors with long-term investment horizons, including institutional investors or high-net-worth individuals, who are willing and able to bear the unique risks involved may be in a good position to take advantage of the VRP and potentially harvest superior risk-adjusted, long-term returns. The VRP provides another unique source of risk and return that investors can access, and one that has the potential to improve the efficiency of diversified portfolios. To access the VRP, our preferred vehicle is the Stone Ridge All Asset Variance Risk Premium Interval Fund (AVRPX). It provides exposure to the VRP across global markets and multiple asset classes, using patient trading strategies to act as a provider, rather than a taker, of liquidity.

CHAPTER 8:
AQR STYLE PREMIA
ALTERNATIVE FUND

Traditional mutual funds are long-only, allowing investors to capture only a portion of the factor premium to which they are seeking. In general, research shows that about half a factor's premium comes from its long side and half from its short side. Let's consider an example, for illustrative purposes only. The value factor is the average annual return on the top 30 percent of stocks ranked by book-to-market ratio (value stocks) minus the average annual return on the bottom 30 percent of stocks (growth stocks). The middle 40 percent are core stocks. About half the value premium comes from the outperformance, relative to core equities, of stocks in the top 30 percent and about half of it comes from the underperformance of stocks in the bottom 30 percent. To earn the full value premium, investors would have to be long value stocks and short growth stocks.

To give investors an alternative that would provide greater exposure to factor premiums than long-only funds, as well as greater diversification benefits, AQR Capital Management created the Style

Premia Alternative Fund (QSPRX). QSPRX is a long-short fund that invests across four styles (or factors), each of which has support in the academic literature. Being both long and short allows investors to achieve greater exposure to factors that have delivered premiums, without also gaining any net exposure to market beta (equity risk). Each of the four styles (value, momentum, carry and defensive) is backed by both economic theory and decades of data on long-term performance across geographies and asset groups.

Further support for factor-based investing strategies comes from Antti Ilmanen and our colleague, Jared Kizer, in their paper, "The Death of Diversification Has Been Greatly Exaggerated," which appeared in the Spring 2012 edition of *The Journal of Portfolio Management*. The paper, which won the prestigious Bernstein Fabozzi/Jacobs Levy Award for best paper of the year, made the case that factor diversification has been much more effective at reducing portfolio volatility and market directionality than asset class diversification.

Let's take a brief look at the four styles employed by the AQR Style Premia Alternative Fund.

- **Value:** The tendency for relatively cheap assets to outperform relatively expensive ones. It is implemented across stocks, industries, bonds, interest rates, currencies and commodities.

- **Cross-Sectional Momentum:** The tendency for an asset's recent relative performance to continue into the near future. It is implemented across stocks, industries, bonds, interest rates, currencies and commodities. (Cross-sectional momentum is different from times-series momentum, which is based on absolute performance instead of relative performance. More on that in Chapter 9.)

- **Carry:** The tendency for higher-yielding assets to provide larger returns than lower-yielding assets. It is implemented across bonds, interest rates, currencies and commodities. (See Appendix B for a more extensive explanation.)

- **Defensive:** The tendency for lower-risk and higher-quality assets to generate larger risk-adjusted returns. It is implemented across stocks, industries and bonds.

The AQR fund accesses each style through long-short portfolios across multiple asset groups. These groups are:

- **Stocks and industries:** 2,000 stocks and industry portfolios across major markets.

- **Country equity indices:** 20 country indices from developed and emerging markets.

- **Bonds:** 10-year futures in six developed markets.

- **Interest rate futures:** Short-term interest rate futures in five developed markets.

- **Currencies:** 22 currencies in developed and emerging markets.

- **Commodities:** Eight commodities futures.

CORRELATIONS

Not only has each of the styles used in the fund provided a premium, but they all have exhibited low to negative correlations with market beta and to each other. For the period from 1990 through 2013:

- The monthly correlations of the value, momentum, carry and defensive styles to market beta were approximately 0, 0, 0.3 and 0, respectively.

- Relative to bonds, the monthly correlations of the value, momentum, carry and defensive styles were 0, 0.1, 0.1 and 0.2, respectively.

- The monthly correlations of value to the momentum, carry and defensive styles were -0.6, -0.1 and -0.1, respectively.

- The monthly correlations of momentum to the carry and defensive styles were 0.2 and 0.1, respectively.

- The monthly correlation of carry to the defensive style was 0.1.

IMPLEMENTATION

Each strategy is implemented in a systematic manner, using a clearly defined, transparent process. The process employs liquid securities, which helps keep transaction costs low. The historical results demonstrate that, while each style within its asset class (or group) has on its own shown a premium, the diversification benefit leads to a whole that is greater than the sum of its parts. In short, composites perform better than the components. For example, the hypothetical Sharpe ratio for the carry factor from 1990 through 2013 was about 0.7 for fixed income, currencies and commodities. The composite Sharpe ratio for the carry factor across these three asset classes was about 1.2. Note that these Sharpe ratios are based on gross returns, and thus overstate the actual results. However, the important point is that the composite outcomes are superior to component results.

TARGET ALLOCATIONS

The target risk allocations of the fund are:

- 30 percent equities across stocks and industries.

- 20 percent equity indices.

- 20 percent bonds.

- 15 percent currencies.

- 15 percent commodities.

This results in an implied style allocation that is:

- 34 percent value.

- 34 percent momentum.

- 18 percent defensive.

- 14 percent carry.

USE OF LEVERAGE

The fund uses leverage to target an annual volatility of 10 percent. The level of leverage employed is adjusted over time, adapting to market conditions. The expectation is that the fund will produce equity-like returns, but with about half the volatility of the market. Over the long term, the average use of leverage is expected to provide investors with $3 to $4 in both long and short positions for each dollar invested.

EXPECTED RETURN

As with the alternative lending, reinsurance and VRP strategies we have discussed, QSPRX has an equity-like expected return (forecasted at about 7 percent net of fees).[1] However, its expected volatility (10 percent) is only about half that of equities. In addition, the correlation

---

[1] Expected return assumptions are based on statistical modeling and are therefore hypothetical in nature and do not reflect actual investment results. They are not a guarantee of future results.

of its return to traditional stock and bond returns is expected to be low. This makes QSPRX an excellent diversifier, reducing tail risk relative to long-only portfolios.

LOCATION

Due to its relatively high turnover and the tax treatment of futures, the fund generally should be considered for tax-advantaged accounts.

SUMMARY

Niels Pedersen, Sébastien Page and Fei He, authors of the study "Asset Allocation: Risk Models for Alternative Investments," concluded that risk premiums diversify more efficiently than traditional alternative investments. They also concluded that the returns of an equally dollar-weighted risk premium portfolio are comparable to those of an endowment portfolio (with allocations to venture capital and hedge funds) except with far less risk.

On an interesting note, the authors cited two studies that found a simple, 1/N diversification strategy (equal-weighting the factors it diversified across) was as good as any of the other methods they tested. This type of strategy is referred to as risk parity.

CHAPTER 9:
TIME-SERIES MOMENTUM

As you may recall, time-series momentum examines the trend of an asset with respect to its own past performance. For that reason, it is often referred to as trend-following. Strategies that attempt to capture the return premium offered by time-series momentum are often called "managed futures," as they take long and short positions in assets via futures markets — ideally in a multitude of futures markets around the globe.

Time-series momentum is different from cross-sectional momentum, which compares the performance of an asset relative to another asset, and has just as much, if not greater, support in the academic literature.

THE EVIDENCE

AQR Capital Management's Brian Hurst, Yao Hua Ooi and Lasse Pedersen, authors of the 2017 paper "A Century of Evidence on Trend-Following Investing," an update of their 2014 study, constructed an equal-weighted
combination of one-month, three-month and 12-month time-series

momentum strategies for 67 markets across four major asset classes (29 commodities, 11 equity indices, 15 bond markets and 12 currency pairs) for the period from January 1880 to December 2016. Their results include implementation costs based on estimates of trading expenses in these four asset classes. They further assumed management fees of 2 percent of asset value plus 20 percent of profits, the traditional "2/20" fee for hedge funds. The following is a summary of their findings:

- Performance was remarkably consistent over an extended time horizon that included the Great Depression, multiple recessions and expansions, multiple wars, stagflation, the global financial crisis of 2008, and periods of rising and falling interest rates.

- Annualized gross returns were 18.0 percent over the full period, with net returns (after fees) of 11.0 percent, higher than the return for equities but with approximately half the volatility (an annual standard deviation of 9.7 percent).

- Net returns were positive in every decade, with the lowest net return, at 4.1 percent, coming in the period beginning in 1919. Net returns were in the single digits over seven of the 14 decades in the period.

- There was virtually no correlation to either stocks or bonds. Thus, the strategy provides a strong diversification benefit. After considering all costs and the 2/20 hedge fund fee, the Sharpe ratio was still 0.76. Even if future returns are not as strong, the diversification benefits would justify an allocation to the strategy.

Hurst, Ooi and Pedersen write that "a large body of research has shown that price trends exist in part due to long-standing behavioral biases exhibited by investors, such as anchoring and herding [and we would add to that list the disposition effect and confirmation bias], as well as the trading activity of non-profit-seeking participants, such as central banks and corporate hedging programs." They observe, for instance, that "when central banks intervene to reduce currency and interest-rate volatility, they slow down the rate at which information is incorporated into prices, thus creating trends."

Hurst, Ooi and Pedersen continued: "The fact that trend-following strategies have performed well historically indicates that these behavioral biases and non-profit-seeking market participants have likely existed for a long time."

They noted that trend-following has done particularly well in extreme up or down years for the stock market, including the most recent global financial crisis of 2008. In fact, the authors found that during the 10 largest drawdowns experienced by the traditional 60 percent stock/40 percent bond portfolio over the 137 years covered in their study, the time-series momentum strategy delivered positive returns in eight of these stress periods, and it delivered significant positive returns in a number of those.

While Hurst, Ooi and Pedersen provided results that included a 2/20 fee structure, today funds with much lower, although still not exactly cheap, expense ratios are available. The authors' firm, AQR, has found that, in implementing time-series momentum strategies, their actual trading costs have been only about one-sixth of the estimates used in the study for much of the sample period (1880 through 1992) and approximately one-half of the estimates used for the more recent period (1993 through 2002).

Hurst, Ooi and Pedersen demonstrate that the time-series momentum premium has been persistent across time and economic regimes, is pervasive across asset classes, is robust to various definitions, has low correlation to other factors, and is implementable.

SUPPORTING EVIDENCE

The preceding findings are consistent with those from prior research, such as the 2013 study by Akindynos-Nikolaos Baltas and Robert Kosowski, "Momentum Strategies in Futures Markets and Trend-Following Funds." Their study covered the period from December 1974 through January 2012 and included 71 futures contracts across several asset classes, specifically 26 commodities, 23 equity indices, seven currencies, and 15 intermediate-term and long-term bonds. The following is a summary of their findings:

- Time-series momentum exhibited strong effects across monthly, weekly and daily frequencies.

- Strategies with different rebalancing frequencies had low cross-correlations, and therefore captured distinct return patterns.

- Times-series momentum patterns were pervasive and fairly robust over the entire evaluation period and within sub-periods.

- Different strategies achieved annualized Sharpe ratios above 1.2 and performed well in both up and down markets, which rendered them good diversifiers in equity bear markets. The fact that different strategies were successful demonstrates time-series momentum's robustness.

- Commodity futures-based momentum strategies had low correlation with other futures strategies. Thus, despite the fact that they had a relatively (compared to the returns of momentum strategies for stocks, bonds and currencies) lower return, they do provide additional diversification benefits.

Importantly, Baltas and Kosowski found that momentum profitability is not limited to illiquid contracts. Rather, momentum strategies are typically implemented by means of exchange-traded futures contracts and forward contracts, which are considered relatively liquid and have relatively low transaction costs compared to cash, equity or bond markets. In fact, they found that "for most of the assets, the demanded number of contracts for the construction of the strategy does not exceed the contemporaneous open interest reported by the Commodity Futures Trading Commission (CFTC) over the period 1986 to 2011." The authors also found that the "notional amount invested in futures contracts in this hypothetical scenario is a small fraction of the global [over-the-counter] derivatives markets (2.3% for commodities, 0.2% for currencies, 2.9% for equities and 0.9% for interest rates at end of 2011)." Thus, they concluded: "Our analyses based on the performance-flow regressions and the hypothetical open interest exceedance scenario do not find statistically or economically significant evidence of capacity constraints in time-series momentum strategies."

We see the findings presented by Baltas and Kosowski again demonstrate that time-series momentum has been persistent, pervasive and robust, as well as that it provides diversification benefits and is implementable. We find further support for the factor in the 2014 study, "Is This Time Different? Trend Following and Financial Crises."

Using almost a century of data on trend-following, the authors, Mark Hutchinson and John O'Brien, investigated what happened to the performance of the strategy subsequent to the U.S. subprime and Eurozone crises, and whether it was typical of what occurs after a financial crisis. But, as Hutchinson and O'Brien observed, identifying a sample of global and regional financial crises can be problematic. Thus, they chose to use the list from two of the most highly cited studies on financial crises, "Manias, Panics, and Crashes: A History of Financial Crises" (originally published in 1978 by Robert Aliber and Charles Kindleberger) and "This Time Is Different: Eight Centuries of Financial Folly" (originally published in 2009 by Carmen Reinhart and Kenneth Rogoff). The six global crises Hutchinson and O'Brien studied were: the Great Depression of 1929, the 1973 Oil Crisis, the Third World Debt Crisis of 1981, the Crash of October 1987, the bursting of the dot-com bubble in 2000 and the Subprime/Euro Crisis beginning in 2007. The regional crises they studied (with the year of inception in parentheses) were: Spain (1977), Norway (1987), Nordic (1989), Japan (1990), Mexico (1994), Asia (1997), Colombia (1997) and Argentina (2000). The start date for each crisis was the month following the equity market high preceding it. Because neither of the two studies Hutchinson and O'Brien used for their list furnished guidance on the length or end date of each crisis, rather than attempting to define when each individual crisis concluded, the authors instead focused on two fixed time periods: 24 months and 48 months after the prior equity market high. Hutchinson and O'Brien's dataset for their global analysis consisted of 21 commodities, 13 government bonds, 21 equity indices and currency crosses derived from nine underlying exchange rates covering a sample period from January 1921 to June 2013. Their results incorporate trading cost estimates as well as the typical 2/20 hedge fund fee. The following is a summary of their findings:

- Time-series momentum has been highly successful over the long term. The average net return for the global portfolio from 1925 to 2013 was 12.1 percent, with volatility of 11 percent. The Sharpe ratio was an impressive 1.1 (a finding consistent with other research).

- A breakdown in futures market return predictability occurred during crisis periods.

- In no-crisis periods, market returns exhibited strong serial correlation at lags of up to 12 months.

- Subsequent to a global financial crisis, trend-following performance tended to be weak for four years on average. This lack of time-series return predictability reduces the opportunity for trend-following to generate returns.

- Comparing the performance of crisis and no-crisis periods, the average return (4.0 percent) in the 24 months following the start of a crisis was less than one-third the return (13.6 percent) earned in no-crisis periods. Performance in the 48 months following the start of a crisis (6.0 percent) was well under half the return (14.9 percent) in no-crisis periods.

- Results were consistent across stocks, bonds and currencies. The exception was commodities, where returns were of similar magnitude in both pre-crisis and post-crisis periods.

- A similar effect appeared when examining portfolios formed of local assets during regional financial crises.

The authors noted that behavioral models link momentum to investor overconfidence and decreasing risk aversion, with both leading to return predictability in asset prices. Under these models, overconfidence should fall and risk aversion should increase following market declines, so it seems logical that return predictability would drop after a financial crisis. It is also important to note, as the authors did, that "governments have an increased tendency to intervene in financial markets during crises, resulting in discontinuities in price patterns." Such interventions can lead to sharp reversals, with negative consequences for trend-following strategies.

Hutchinson and O'Brien concluded that the performance of trend-following strategies is "much weaker in crisis periods, where performance can be as little as one-third of that in normal market conditions." They continue, writing: "This result is supported by our evidence for regional crises, though the effect seems to be more short-lived. In our analysis of the underlying markets, our empirical evidence indicates a breakdown in the time series predictability, pervasive in normal market conditions, on which trend following relies."

SUMMARY

As an investment style, trend-following has existed for a long time. Data from the aforementioned research provides strong out-of-sample evidence beyond the substantial evidence that already existed in the literature. It also provides consistent, long-term evidence that trends have been pervasive features of global stock, bond, commodity and currency markets.

Regarding whether we should expect trends to continue, as AQR's Hurst, Ooi and Pedersen concluded, "the most likely candidates to explain why markets have tended to trend more often than not include investors' behavioral biases, market frictions, hedging demands, and market interventions by central banks and governments. Such market interventions and hedging programs are still prevalent, and investors are likely to continue to suffer from the same behavioral biases that have influenced price behavior over the past century, setting the stage for trend-following investing going forward."

IMPLEMENTING THE STRATEGY

To gain access to the time-series momentum factor, our preferred vehicles are two funds managed by AQR Capital Management: the AQR Managed Futures Fund (AQMRX) and the AQR Managed Futures High Volatility Fund (QMHRX). As with the AQR Style Premia Alternative Fund, the managed futures funds provide exposure to time-series momentum across four asset classes: equity indices, bonds, commodities and currencies. These funds diversify risk through exposure to more than 100 liquid futures and forward contracts.

AQMRX has an expected return similar to U.S. equities and is managed to a 10 percent volatility level. QMHRX is managed to a 15 percent volatility level, with proportionally higher forward-looking return expectations. Their expense ratios are 1.15 percent and 1.58 percent, respectively.

CHAPTER 10:
HOW MUCH TO ALLOCATE
TO ALTERNATIVES?

Just as there is no right answer to how much an investor should "tilt" their portfolio to factors such as size and value, there is no right answer to how much an investor should allocate to alternatives. With that said, we believe there is a good way to think about the question. We begin with the basic assumption that, while markets are not perfectly efficient, they are highly efficient. In efficient markets, all risky assets should deliver similar risk-adjusted returns. Because this is the case, all else being equal, investors should not prefer one investment risk to another. (Note that all else is not always equal. For example, if your labor capital correlates highly with an investment risk, you should consider underweighting that risk in your portfolio.) That leads us to conclude a risk parity type of portfolio is a good starting point. Current stock valuations play an important role in determining future returns. Thus, they (not historical returns) should be used to help determine a portfolio's expected return. The Shiller CAPE 10 is a useful metric to help estimate future returns.

RISK PARITY

The risk parity approach to asset allocation focuses on the amount of risk in each portfolio component rather than the specific dollar amount invested in each portfolio component. In other words, it emphasizes not the allocation of capital (like traditional models), but on the allocation of risk. Consider the following example.

While the typical 60 percent stock/40 percent bond portfolio has 60 percent of its dollars allocated to equities, because stocks are so much more volatile than safe Treasury bonds, about 80 percent to 90 percent of the portfolio's risk is equity risk. Broadly diversified equity portfolios historically have experienced volatility (as measured by the annual standard deviation of returns) of about 20 percent. This compares to volatility of about 5 percent for a high-quality intermediate-term bond portfolio with an average maturity of five years. Thus, if we consider how much risk (as measured by volatility) we have allocated to stocks and bonds, we see the following:

- Equity Risk: 60 x 20 = 1,200

- Bond Risk: 40 x 5 = 200

- Total Risk: 1,200 + 200 = 1,400

- Percentage Equity Risk: 1,200/1,400 = 86 percent

As you recall from our discussion of how to build more efficient portfolios, adding more exposure to the size and value factors allows investors to lower their overall allocation to stocks (and, thus, market beta) and increase their allocation to safer bonds. This is possible because the stocks they do own have higher expected returns than the market. The result is more of a risk parity portfolio. Let's explore another example to illustrate this point.

Once again, Portfolio A is the typical 60 percent stock/40 percent bond portfolio. Portfolio B reduces its stock allocation to 40 percent, but substitutes the DFA U.S. Small Cap Value Portfolio (DFSVX) for the Vanguard Total (U.S.) Stock Market Index Fund (VTSMX). The increased exposure to the size and value factors, with their higher expected returns, allows us to increase its exposure to safe bonds from 40 percent to 60 percent. Our example covers the period from April 1993 (chosen because it is the inception date of DFA's small-cap value fund) through December 2016.

- Portfolio A: 60 percent Vanguard Total (U.S.) Stock Market Index Fund (VTSMX)/40 percent Vanguard Intermediate-Term Treasury Fund (VFITX)

- Portfolio B: 40 percent DFA U.S. Small Cap Value Portfolio (DFSVX)/60 percent Vanguard Intermediate-Term Treasury Fund (VFITX)

The table on the next page presents Portfolio A and Portfolio B's exposure to the market beta, size, value, quality (discussed in Appendix B) and term factors. The figures inside the parentheses indicate the utilized mutual fund's exposure to (or loading on) each factor. To calculate the portfolio's factor exposure, the figures found to the left of the parentheses, multiply the fund's loading by the allocation percentage. For example, over the sample period, DFSVX had a loading of 0.65 on the value factor. Portfolio B's 40 percent allocation to DFSVX results in a value factor loading for the entire portfolio of 0.26 (40 percent x 0.65). Data comes from the regression tool available at the website www.portfoliovisualizer.com.

APRIL 1993–DECEMBER 2016

	PORTFOLIO A*	PORTFOLIO B*
ANNUALIZED RETURNS (%)	7.9	8.6
STANDARD DEVIATION	8.8	7.5
MARKET BETA	0.60 (1.00)	0.42 (1.04)
SIZE	-0.01 (-0.01)	0.32 (0.82)
VALUE	0.01 (0.01)	0.26 (0.65)
QUALITY	0.01 (0.01)	0.03 (0.07)
TERM	0.17 (0.41)	0.23 (0.41)

*Annualized return information is provided to show the benefits of factor diversification and does not reflect the performance of an actual portfolio and does not reflect any advisory fees or trading costs incurred in the management of an actual portfolio. Performance is historical and does not guarantee future results.

As you can see, while the two portfolios had relatively similar returns and volatility, Portfolio B was more efficient in both respects. In addition, Portfolio A had a 0.60 loading on market beta, just a 0.17 loading on the term factor, and negligible exposure to the other factors. Portfolio B was far more diversified, with relatively more equal weightings on the other factors. Portfolios can also be structured to gain exposure to the momentum factor, though neither of these portfolios are. A portfolio with even greater risk parity can be constructed through the use of long-short funds.

The benefits of diversifying across factors and creating a portfolio with greater risk parity are apparent in the following table. The data for the market beta, size, value and momentum factors covers the period from 1927 through 2016. We have included two additional factors, profitability (data begins in 1964) and quality (data begins in 1958), both of which are discussed in Appendix B. The table presents each factor's premium, volatility and Sharpe ratio. It also shows the same information for three naïve 1/N portfolios. Portfolio 1 (P1) is allocated 25 percent to each of four factors: market beta, size, value and momentum. Portfolio 2 (P2) is allocated 20 percent to each of the same four factors, but adds a 20 percent allocation to the profitability factor. Portfolio 3 (P3) is allocated the same way, but substitutes the quality factor for the profitability factor.

FACTOR DIVERSIFICATION 1927–2016

	MEAN RETURN	STANDARD DEVIATION	SHARPE RATIO
MARKET BETA	8.4	20.5	0.41
SIZE	3.3	13.9	0.24
VALUE	5.1	14.2	0.36
MOMENTUM	9.3	15.9	0.58
PROFITABILITY*	3.0	9.6	0.31
QUALITY**	4.0	9.8	0.41
P1	6.5	8.8	0.74
P2*	5.3	5.5	0.96
P3**	5.6	5.0	1.12

Data supplied by Fama/French Data Library and AQR Capital Management. Indices are not available for direct investment. Their performance does not reflect expenses associated with the management of an actual portfolio, nor do indices represent results of actual trading. Information is from sources deemed reliable, but its accuracy cannot be guaranteed. Performance is historical and does not guarantee future results.

*1964-2016 **1958-2016

As you review the data in the preceding table, note that the three portfolios' Sharpe ratios are dramatically higher than the Sharpe ratios of any individual factor. This is a direct result of each factor's low correlation with the others, and demonstrates the benefits of diversifying across unique sources of risk. The table below shows the annual correlations of the market beta, size, value, momentum, profitability and quality factors over the period from 1964 through 2016.

ANNUAL CORRELATIONS 1964–2016

FACTOR	MARKET BETA	SIZE	VALUE	MOMENTUM	PROFITABILITY	QUALITY
MARKET BETA	1.00	0.28	-0.23	-0.18	-0.28	-0.52
SIZE	0.28	1.00	0.01	-0.13	-0.22	-0.52
VALUE	-0.23	0.01	1.00	-0.21	0.09	0.04
MOMENTUM	-0.18	-0.13	-0.21	1.00	0.03	0.27
PROFITABILITY	-0.28	-0.22	0.09	0.03	1.00	0.73
QUALITY	-0.52	-0.52	0.04	0.27	0.73	1.00

Note that with the sole exception of the high correlation between the related profitability and quality factors (which we should expect because profitability is one of the traits of quality companies), correlations are low to negative. Notice in particular the negative correlations of the momentum premium to the beta, size and value premiums. This demonstrates the diversification benefit of adding momentum factor exposure to a portfolio that incorporates these other factors.

We can also see the benefits of diversifying across factors in the following table, which shows the odds of underperformance (that is, the odds of producing a negative return) over various time horizons.

ODDS OF UNDERPERFORMANCE 1927–2016

	1-YEAR	3-YEAR	5-YEAR	10-YEAR	20-YEAR
MARKET BETA	34	24	18	10	3
SIZE	41	34	30	23	14
VALUE	36	27	21	13	5
MOMENTUM	28	16	10	3	0
PROFITABILITY*	38	29	24	16	8
QUALITY**	34	24	18	10	3
P1	23	10	5	1	0
P2*	17	5	2	0	0
P3**	13	3	1	0	0

Data supplied by Fama/French Data Library and AQR Capital Management. Indices are not available for direct investment. Their performance does not reflect expenses associated with the management of an actual portfolio, nor do indices represent results of actual trading. Information is from sources deemed reliable, but its accuracy cannot be guaranteed. Performance is historical and does not guarantee future results.

*1964-2015 **1958-2015

In each case, the longer the horizon, the lower the odds of a negative result become. However, no matter how long the horizon, each of the individual factors still experienced some periods of underperformance, even at 20 years. The sole exception is momentum at the 20-year period. Even this outcome, though, does not guarantee future success for momentum at that horizon.

The key takeaway from the tables and data in this chapter is that diversification across unique sources of risk and return has resulted in more efficient portfolios. That, or course, brings us to the alternative investments we have discussed, and the impact of an allocation to them.

ADDING ALTERNATIVES

Like with factors, adding alternatives that represent unique sources of risk and return and that offer equity-like expected returns should allow us to lower a portfolio's allocation to market beta (the riskiest factor), thus creating portfolios with even greater risk parity and even more diversified sources of risk. Because each of the alternatives we have discussed shows low correlations to other portfolio assets, we should end up with a more efficient portfolio — one with similar returns but less risk.

HOW MUCH TO ALLOCATE TO ALTERNATIVES?

We offer this suggestion: Investors should consider an allocation to the alternatives we recommend of at least a 10 percent and up to 30 percent. With that said, because most alternatives are not tax efficient, many investors may be constrained in their ability to include them in their portfolios due to limited capacity in tax-advantaged accounts.

You can use the following hypothetical, which is based on the concept of risk parity and the hypothesis that all risky assets should have similar risk-adjusted returns, as a starting point when contemplating a specific allocation to our recommended alternatives. Because all risky assets should earn similar risk-adjusted returns, investors should not prefer one alternative over another. As a result, assume you have decided to include an allocation to four of the alternatives we have discussed: alternative lending, reinsurance, the variance risk premium and the AQR Style Premia Alternative Fund. You might choose to commit one-fourth of your total alternatives allocation to each of the four strategies. If you would then also like to include an allocation to time-series momentum using AQR's managed futures funds, consider this: Instead of thinking about it as a fifth alternative, consider it a fifth factor beyond the four to which the AQR Style Premia Alternative Fund already provides exposure. Thus, if you had decided that you wanted a 25 percent allocation to alternatives, you might allot 6 percent to each of the alternative lending, reinsurance and variance risk premium strategies. You would next include a 4.8 percent allocation (0.8 x 6 percent) to the AQR Style Premia Alternative Fund and a 1.2 percent allocation (0.2 x 6 percent) to a managed futures strategy.

FROM WHERE SHOULD THE ALLOCATION TO ALTERNATIVES COME?

Whenever we add an investment to a portfolio, it must reduce the allocation to other assets. The question that arises is whether an allocation to alternative strategies should come from stocks or bonds. Because the expected return to each of the alternatives we have considered is equity-like (about 7 percent), and given that their volatility is much lower (about one-quarter to one-half the 20 percent volatility of equities), investors with relatively high equity allocations (more than 60 percent) should consider taking an allocation to alternatives from their equity holdings. On the other hand, because the volatility of an equal-weighted portfolio of alternatives is expected to be about 6 percent (compared to about 5 percent for an intermediate-term, high-quality bond strategy), and given their equity-like expected return, investors with relatively low equity allocations (less than 40 percent) should consider taking an allocation to alternatives from their bond holdings. If you decide to do the latter, it is important to recognize that in return for significantly higher expected return, the left tail risk of your portfolio has now increased. Investors with equity allocations between 40 percent and 60 percent can consider taking the allocation pro rata from the two.

CONCLUSION

We hope you have found your journey with us both informative and of great value. After all, the holy grail of investing is the search for investment strategies that can deliver higher expected returns without increased risk, or the same expected return with reduced risk. We have attempted to give you the road map to it. Clearly, the way evolved since the publication of the original version of this book in 2014. New alternatives have become available, allowing us to create even more efficient strategies that improve the odds of achieving your financial goals while also greatly reducing the risk of outliving your assets. The road map comes with the following "directions."

Current stock valuations play an important role in determining future returns. Thus, they (not historical returns) should be used to help determine a portfolio's expected return. The Shiller CAPE 10 is a useful metric to help estimate future returns.

Consider the expected return only the mean of a wide dispersion of potential returns. Your plan should incorporate options (such as staying in the workforce longer, moving to a location with a lower cost of living, and so on) that you will adopt to minimize the risk of failure, regardless of which potential outcome becomes reality.

Think about diversification in terms of the factors (rather than asset classes) that explain returns, diversifying risk across those factors as well as the other unique sources of risk we have discussed.

To the extent you are willing to accept the risk of tracking error regret, concentrate the equity portion of your portfolio in the highest expected returning factors. All else equal (for example, expense ratios), use funds that have the highest loadings on (exposure to) the factors in which you want to invest. That allows you to minimize your exposure to market beta, which is the biggest risk factor.

Diversify your portfolio across the globe. For example, the portfolio's equity portion might have a 50 percent allocation to U.S. small value stocks, a 37.5 percent allocation to international developed markets small value stocks and a 12.5 percent allocation to emerging markets value stocks. These percentages reflect current geographical market weightings.

We also offer an important caution. Just as we can only estimate the stock market's future expected return, we can only estimate the future return to small value stocks. History and current valuations provide a guide, helping us make estimates. However, all crystal balls are cloudy — there are no guarantees. What we do know is that a low-market-beta/high-tilt portfolio does reduce the risk of fat tails (both good and bad). We cannot guarantee, though, that it will produce the same return as a more market-like portfolio with a higher equity allocation.

Your journey with us is not quite over. The book's appendices address the following six important topics:

- The use of Monte Carlo simulations in determining your asset allocation.

- Since Eugene Fama and Kenneth French's work on their three-factor model, academics have "discovered" other factors that not only help explain the differences in returns of diversified portfolios, but also carry premiums. Among the additional factors we believe investors should consider are cross-sectional momentum, profitability, quality and carry (one of the four factors in the AQR Style Premia Alternative Fund).

- Not all index and passively managed funds are created equal. Even two passively managed funds within the same asset class (such as U.S. small value) can have very different portfolio construction rules that lead to different loadings on factors, and different expected returns.

- The role of REITs in a diversified portfolio.

- The importance of knowing when you have "enough."

- Recommended investment vehicles.

APPENDIX A:
MONTE CARLO SIMULATIONS

In "traditional" retirement planning, annual investment returns are assumed to be a constant number, such as 6 percent per year. Retirement planners arrive at this number based on a portfolio's asset allocation and on assumptions about the returns of various investments. Outcomes using this computation typically are presented as expected wealth values over the anticipated period of retirement.

The problem with this approach is that investment returns are not deterministic. While investing is about risk, retirement calculators that present single scenarios treat outcomes either as a certainty or, at best, a 50/50 proposition (for instance, the odds are 50/50 that you will do better or worse than the expected result). Investing is not a science in the same way physics is. No one knows with precision, beforehand, what the return of different investments will be over any given number of years. Investment returns are random variables, characterized by expected values (averages), standard deviations and, more generally, probability distributions. For this reason, projections of an investment program's possible results should also be expressed in terms of probabilities. For example, an expected outcome should be presented in terms such as:

- There is a 95 percent chance you will not run out of money in retirement.

- There is a 50 percent probability you will accumulate at least $3.1 million.

- There is a 25 percent chance you will accumulate $5.2 million or more. But, there is also a 10 percent chance you will accumulate only $400,000 or less.

To arrive at this type of conclusion, it is necessary to use a tool known as a Monte Carlo (MC) simulation.

MC simulations require a set of assumptions regarding time horizon, initial investment, asset allocation, withdrawals, savings, retirement income, rate of inflation, correlation among different asset classes and — very importantly — the return distributions of the portfolio.

In MC simulation programs, the growth of an investment portfolio is determined by two important inputs: portfolio average expected return and portfolio volatility, represented by the standard deviation measure. Based on these two inputs, the MC simulation program generates a sequence of random returns from which one return is applied in each incremental period (typically one year) of the simulation. This process is repeated thousands of times to calculate the likelihood of possible outcomes and their potential distributions.

MC simulations also provide another important benefit: They allow investors to view the outcomes of various strategies and how marginal adjustments in asset allocation change the odds of these outcomes. We will examine the results for a hypothetical investor who begins with a $1 million portfolio. An initial withdrawal is made equal to the specified withdrawal rate multiplied by the $1 million starting value. The remaining assets then grow or shrink per the asset returns in the replication for that year. At the end of the year, the portfolio is rebalanced back to investor's target allocation. In subsequent years, the withdrawal is the prior year's withdrawal plus inflation for that year. Withdrawals are made at the start of each year. It is assumed that taxes are included in the withdrawal amount.

The following table shows the real return capital market assumptions used in the MC simulation. It is important to note that the results from any MC simulation will be based on its inputs. If we were to use different capital market assumptions, the results in the tables that follow would be very different. We build capital market assumptions using current valuations and yields, so these assumptions will change over time.

CAPITAL MARKET ASSUMPTIONS

	ARITHMETIC MEAN REAL RETURN (%)	ANNUAL STANDARD DEVIATION (%)
TOTAL STOCK MARKET EQUITY	4.6	17.3
TILTED EQUITY PORTFOLIO	6.8	20.0
FIXED INCOME	0.8	4.2
INFLATION	2.0	N/A

This section will look at portfolios with various hypothetical allocations. The success rate is defined as the probability that the portfolio has at least one dollar at the end of the planning horizon. Of course, if someone has a 95 percent success rate, this also means that investor has a 5 percent chance of failure. Outcomes are calculated over a 30-year horizon. We will review the results using three different initial withdrawal rates: 3 percent, 4 percent and 5 percent. A 4 percent withdrawal rate on a $1 million starting portfolio indicates that $40,000 is withdrawn in the first year, and then adjusted for inflation thereafter.

- **Portfolio A:** 60 percent total stock market/40 percent fixed income

- **Portfolio B:** 60 percent equity tilted to small-cap and value/40 percent fixed income

- **Portfolio C:** 40 percent equity tilted to small-cap and value/60 percent fixed income

The equity portion of the portfolios tilted to small-cap and value stocks have loadings of 0.5 on the size factor and 0.2 on the value factor.

ODDS OF SUCCESS (%)

	3% WITHDRAWAL RATE	4% WITHDRAWAL RATE	5% WITHDRAWAL RATE
PORTFOLIO A	93	70	40
PORTFOLIO B	96	81	58
PORTFOLIO C	98	80	43

At a relatively low 3 percent withdrawal rate, changes in asset allocation do not have a significant effect on success rates. However, by making such a change, an investor could slightly improve the odds of success while reducing the portfolio's equity allocation. At a 4 percent withdrawal rate, we see significant improvement in success rates by tilting the equity portion of the portfolio to small-cap and value stocks. At a relatively high 5 percent withdrawal rate, no amount of changes in the asset allocation will get the investor to an acceptable success rate. This investor should reduce their spending, plan on working longer, lower their goal or find other sources of income.

We will now examine how adding the alternative investments we have discussed to Portfolio B (60 percent equity tilted to small-cap and value stocks/40 percent fixed income) affect the odds of success.

IMPACT OF ADDING ALTERNATIVES

We will replace 15 percent of Portfolio B's 60 percent equity allocation with alternatives (Portfolio B1). We will use a naïve 1/N allocation. Thus, our five alternatives, the AQR Style Premia Alternative Fund (QSPRX), the AQR Managed Futures High Volatility Fund (QMHRX), the Stone Ridge Alternative Lending Risk Premium Interval Fund (LENDX), the Stone Ridge Reinsurance Risk Premium Interval Fund (SRRIX) and the Stone Ridge All Asset Variance Risk Premium Interval Fund (AVRPX), each receive 3 percent. We will also replace 25 percent of Portfolio B's 60 percent equity allocation with alternatives (Portfolio B2). This 25 percent allocation is split equally among the same funds that are in Portfolio B1, each receiving 5 percent. It is important to note that these allocations are simply for illustrative purposes (though they are consistent with our belief in efficient markets and that all risky assets should have similar expected returns). Changing the weights within the alternatives allocation or changing their mix does not significantly change the results. We also would see similar results if we pulled the allocation to alternatives from fixed income instead of from equities. The biggest driver of the change in success rates is the size of the alternatives allocation, not which strategies are selected for inclusion in that part of the portfolio.

ODDS OF SUCCESS (%)

	3% WITHDRAWAL RATE	4% WITHDRAWAL RATE	5% WITHDRAWAL RATE
PORTFOLIO B	96	81	58
PORTFOLIO B1	99	87	61
PORTFOLIO B2	100	92	62

At the 3 percent withdrawal rate, we again see relatively small (but positive) changes in success rates. At a 4 percent withdrawal rate, we see meaningful improvements in success rates. At a 5 percent withdrawal rate, we again fail to see much improvement in success rates. The likely reason for this last outcome is that a 5 percent withdrawal rate is not sustainable (at least at today's fixed income yields and equity valuations).

The combination of tilting the equity portfolio and adding alternatives significantly improves MC simulation success rates. Compared to our starting point, the market-like Portfolio A, Portfolio B1, with a 15 percent allocation to alternatives, improved the odds of success with 3 percent, 4 percent and 5 percent withdrawal rates by 6 percentage points (from 93 percent to 99 percent), 17 percentage points (from 70 percent to 87 percent) and 21 percentage points (from 40 percent to 61 percent), respectively. Let's consider another way to think about this. At a 4 percent withdrawal rate, Portfolio A had a success rate of just 70 percent. Those odds might be unacceptable, forcing you down to the lower 3 percent withdrawal rate. Adding the 15 percent allocation to alternatives improves the odds of success at the higher 4 percent withdrawal rate to 87 percent. If 87 percent was an acceptable success rate to you (if you would still have options you could exercise if left tail risk appeared), you could then increase your withdrawals from 3 percent back to 4 percent, a 33 percent increase in spending over your retirement. Portfolio B2, with a 25 percent allocation to alternatives, improves the odds of success even further (all the way to 92 percent at a 4 percent withdrawal rate).

Adding unique sources of risk that provide an equity-like return changes a portfolio's potential distribution of returns in a favorable way. You can use this knowledge not only to improve the odds of achieving your financial goals, but also to increase your spending during retirement.

APPENDIX B:
OTHER KNOWN SOURCES OF RETURN

MOMENTUM

A cross-sectional momentum-based strategy buys stocks that have done *relatively* well over the past 12 months and shorts stocks that have had relatively poor returns over the same period. Narasimhan Jegadeesh and Sheridan Titman, in their 1993 paper, "Returns to Buying Winners and Selling Losers: Implications for Stock Market Efficiency," which appeared in *The Journal of Finance*, are generally credited in academia for discovering momentum. In this paper, the authors found that recent relative winners (over the previous three to 12 months) will continue to be relative winners over the next three to 12 months, and recent relative losers will continue to be relative losers over the next three to 12 months. They found the effect disappears after 12 months.

In 1994, Cliff Asness, as part of his Ph.D. dissertation titled "Variables that Explain Stock Returns," found long-term winners eventually become growth stocks that underperform and long-term losers eventually become value stocks that outperform. His was one of the first papers that argued value and momentum are related.

In 1996, Eugene Fama and Kenneth French compared all the market anomalies known at the time to their Fama-French three-factor model. They found momentum was the only anomaly to survive and not be captured by the size and value effects.

In 1997, Asness further explored the relationship between value and momentum strategies in a paper published in the CFA Institute's *Financial Analysts Journal*. He found that value tends to be strongest among low-momentum stocks and weakest among high-momentum stocks. He also found that momentum strategies work across the value-versus-growth spectrum.

Also in 1997, Mark Carhart augmented the Fama-French three-factor model with a fourth factor based on momentum. The new momentum factor made a valuable contribution to the explanatory power of the model. In addition, he found that momentum stocks are correlated with each other.

The most commonly cited concern regarding momentum strategies centers around transaction costs. A momentum strategy creates high turnover. This raises the question of whether the momentum premium survives in the "real world" with real trading costs. The 2012 paper "Trading Costs of Asset Pricing Anomalies," authored by Andrea Frazzini, Ronen Israel and Tobias Moskowitz, found that actual trading costs are low enough to allow the momentum premium to survive.

From 1927 through 2016, the average annual cross-sectional momentum premium was 9.3 percent.

PROFITABILITY

A June 2012 study by Robert Novy-Marx, "The Other Side of Value: The Gross Profitability Premium," offered new insights into the cross-section of stocks returns. His data sample covered the period from 1962 through 2010, and employed accounting data for a given fiscal year starting at the end of June of the following calendar year. The following is a summary of Novy-Marx's findings, which have affected the way many value investors (such as Dimensional Fund Advisors) construct portfolios:

- Profitability, as measured by gross profits-to-assets, has roughly the same power as book-to-market ratio (a value measure) in predicting the cross-section of average returns.

- Profitable firms generate significantly higher returns than unprofitable firms, despite having significantly higher valuation ratios (that is, higher price-to-book ratios).

- Profitable firms tend to be growth firms (profitable firms grow faster). Gross profitability is a powerful predictor of future growth in earnings, free cash flow and payouts.

- The most profitable firms earn a 0.31 percent per month higher average return than the least profitable firms. The data is statistically significant (with a t-statistic of 2.49).

- Controlling for profitability dramatically increases the performance of value strategies, especially among the largest, most liquid stocks. Controlling for book-to-market ratio improves the performance of profitability strategies.

- Because both gross profits-to-assets and book-to-market ratios are highly persistent, the strategies' turnover is relatively low.

- Because strategies based on profitability are growth strategies, they provide an excellent hedge for value strategies. Adding profitability on top of a value strategy reduces overall volatility because the two strategies are negatively correlated.

As additional evidence that the two strategies combine well, consider the following: While both profitability and value strategies generally performed well over the study's sample period, both had significant periods in which they lost money. Profitability performed poorly from the mid-1970s to the early 1980s and over the mid-2000s while value performed poorly in the 1990s. However, profitability generally performed well during the periods in which value performed poorly and vice versa. As a result, the mixed profitability/value strategy never experienced a losing five-year period.

In summary, the research has found profitability to be persistent over long periods, pervasive around the globe, robust to various definitions and implementable. From 1964 through 2015, the average annual profitability premium was 3.0 percent.

QUALITY

Building on Novy-Marx's work, researchers have since extended the profitability factor to a broader quality factor (the returns to high-quality companies minus the returns to low-quality companies) that captures a larger set of quality characteristics. While there is no one consistent definition of quality, in general, high-quality companies have the following traits: low earnings volatility, high margins, high asset turnover (indicating the efficient use of assets), low financial leverage, low operating leverage (indicating a strong balance sheet and low macroeconomic risk) and low specific-stock risk (volatility unexplained by macroeconomic activity). Companies with these characteristics historically have provided higher returns, especially in down markets. In particular, high-quality stocks that are profitable, stable, growing and have a high payout ratio outperform low-quality stocks with the opposite characteristics.

Jean-Philippe Bouchaud, Stefano Ciliberti, Augustin Landier, Guillaume Simon and David Thesmar, authors of the study "The Excess Returns of 'Quality' Stocks: A Behavioral Anomaly," which was published in the June 2016 issue of the *Journal of Investment Strategies*, examined the quality factor and found that its performance in the United States for the period from 1990 through 2012 was very strong, producing a Sharpe ratio of 1.2 with a highly significant t-stat of about 6. It was also highly successful in all geographical areas.

From 1958 through 2015, the average annual quality premium was 4.0 percent.

CARRY

The carry factor is the tendency for higher-yielding assets to provide higher returns than lower-yielding assets. It is a cousin to the value factor, which, as you recall, is the tendency for relatively cheap assets to outperform relatively expensive ones. A simplified description of the carry trade is the return an investor receives (net of financing) if asset prices remain the same. The classic application is in currencies (going long the currencies of countries with the highest interest rates and short the currencies of those with the lowest). Currency carry has been both a well-known and productive strategy over several decades. However, the carry trade is a general phenomenon.

Ralph Koijen, Tobias Moskowitz, Lasse Pedersen and Evert Vrugt, authors of the 2015 study "Carry," write: "While the concept of 'carry' has been applied almost exclusively to currencies, it ... can be applied to any asset." They defined carry as the expected return on an asset assuming its price does not change — that is, stock prices do not change, currency yields do not change, bond yields do not change and spot commodity prices remain unchanged. Thus, for equities, the carry trade is defined by the dividend yield (the strategy involves going long countries with high dividend yield and short countries with low dividend yield). For bonds, it is determined by the term structure of rates. For commodities, it is determined by the roll return (the difference between spot rates and future rates).

The authors found a carry trade that goes long high-carry assets and shorts low-carry assets earns significant returns in each asset class they examined with an annualized Sharpe ratio of 0.7 on average. Further, a diversified portfolio of carry strategies across all asset classes (stocks, bonds, commodities and currencies) earns a Sharpe ratio of 1.2. They also found that carry predicts future returns in every asset class with a positive coefficient, but the magnitude of the predictive coefficient differs across asset classes.

Importantly, the research has found that the correlations among carry strategies are low. This reduces the volatility of a diversified portfolio substantially, and mitigates the risks of fat tails associated with all carry trades. While all individual carry strategies have excess kurtosis (fat tails), a carry strategy diversified across all asset classes has skewness close to zero and thinner tails than diversified, passive exposure to the global market.

Lastly, the carry trade has a simple, intuitive rationale because prices balance out supply and demand for capital across markets. In a 2017 study published in *The Journal of Portfolio Management*, Elroy Dimson, Paul Marsh and Mike Staunton found that the average carry premium in stocks across 21 countries was 3.9 percent. Their dataset began between 1900 and 1975, depending on the country, and covered the period through 2016.

SUMMARY

Given the compelling academic evidence, including exposure in your portfolio to the momentum, profitability, quality and carry factors merits consideration. Doing so allows you to create more of a risk parity portfolio further diversified in its sources of risk. It should also be a more efficient portfolio that helps reduce the risk of black swans.

For those interested in a more detailed discussion of these factors, we recommend Larry's book, co-authored with Andrew Berkin, *Your Complete Guide to Factor-Based Investing*.

APPENDIX C: THE ROLE OF REITs IN A DIVERSIFIED PORTFOLIO

Many investors think of real estate investment trusts (REITs) as a distinct asset class because, in aggregate, they historically have had relatively low correlations with both stocks and bonds, and their returns were not well explained by the single-factor CAPM. For example, over the period from January 1978 through May 2017, the Dow Jones U.S. Select REIT Index's monthly correlation with the S&P 500 Index was 0.58, and its monthly correlation with five-year Treasury bonds was just 0.08.

These low correlations, along with the fact that the Dow Jones U.S. Select REIT Index produced a higher return (12.2 percent) than either the S&P 500 Index (11.7 percent) or five-year Treasury bonds (7.1 percent), led many investors to believe that adding REITs to a mixed-asset portfolio expanded the efficient frontier, providing superior risk-adjusted returns.

The evolution of modern financial theory and the development of more sophisticated multi-factor models provide us with tools to evaluate the "traditional" view (which we held until recently) of REITs as both a separate asset class and one that expands the efficient frontier. With that in mind, we will review recent papers that specifically address these issues. The first is a May 2017 study by two of our colleagues, Jared

Kizer of Buckingham Strategic Wealth and The BAM ALLIANCE and Sean Grover.

Motivated by the observation that a lot of previous research treated REITs as a distinct asset class based on correlation alone, they decided to take another look at REITs in their own study, "Are REITs a Distinct Asset Class?" Their data sample covered the period from January 1978 through September 2016.

Kizer and Grover began by establishing criteria that an asset class must meet for it to be considered distinct. These criteria are:

1. Low correlation with established asset classes, such as broad market equities and government bonds.

2. Statistically significant positive alpha (outperformance) with respect to generally accepted factor models.

3. Inability to be replicated by a long-only portfolio holding established asset classes.

4. Improved mean-variance frontier when added to a portfolio holding established asset classes.

Prior research had shown that, in terms of equity risk, REITs have significant exposure not only to market beta, but also to the size and value factors. In addition, they have been shown to have exposure to the term premium. In their analysis, Kizer and Grover employed a six-factor model comprising the market beta, size, value and momentum equity factors as well as the term and credit bond factors. The credit factor (referred to as IGDEF) subtracts the return of a duration-matched portfolio of Treasury bonds from the total return of the investment-grade corporate bond index to isolate the return premium associated with the weaker credit of corporate bonds.

Their regression analysis included not only REITs, but also 12 other industries available on Ken French's website. The following is a summary of their findings:

- Demonstrating the explanatory power of the six-factor model, virtually all industries, including REITS, are well explained by the four equity factors and two fixed income factors. Only one industry category (a catch-all that included mining, construction, transportation, entertainment and hospitality, among other sectors) had statistically significant annualized alpha, and the estimate was negative.

- The annual alpha estimate for REITs was -0.89 percent with a t-statistic (t-stat) near zero (-0.3).

- REITs showed statistically significant exposures to market beta (0.61 with a t-stat of 10.2), size (0.44 with a t-stat of 6.1) and value (0.77 with a t-stat of 9.9), as well as a small negative (-0.08) and statistically insignificant (t-stat of -1.7) exposure to the momentum factor, a large (0.70) and statistically significant (t-stat of 3.8) exposure to the term premium, and a large (0.92) and statistically significant (t-stat of 3.9) exposure to the credit (default) premium.

- While the R-squared ratio (which measures how well a factor model explains returns) was relatively low for REITs (0.51), this was also true for several other industries, including energy, utilities and health care.

These findings led Kizer and Grover to conclude that, while the low R-squared ratios cited in the last bullet point indicate diversifiable risks present in each industry, they do not also indicate uniqueness in underlying return drivers. They state: "While the relatively low correlation with the S&P 500 Index and 5YT [five-year Treasury bonds] was encouraging, the four- and six-factor regression models indicate that REITs are likely not a distinct asset class, especially when compared to the results of other industries." Their evidence demonstrates that, while REITs may meet the first of the four criteria they established (low correlation), they fail to meet the second (significant alpha).

Kizer and Grover next tested REITs against their third criteria — a distinct asset class should not be easily replicated by a long-only portfolio of established asset classes. Given the factor exposures they had found, and using returns for U.S. small-cap value stocks (SV) from Ken French's data library and the Barclays long-term corporate bond index (CORP), they attempted to replicate REIT returns with these two returns series.

The following table shows the results of a portfolio allocating about 67 percent to SV and 33 percent to CORP. This optimal (in the sense that it displayed the best fit using historical data) replicating portfolio had a monthly correlation with REITs of 0.72. The table also presents other statistics that compare the optimal replicating portfolio to REITs over the period from January 1978 through September 2016.

MONTHLY RETURN SUMMARY STATISTICS
(JANUARY 1978–SEPTEMBER 2016)

	REITs	PORTFOLIO
AVERAGE RETURN (%)	1.13	1.20
COMPOUND RETURN (%)	12.5	14.3
STANDARD DEVIATION (%)	18.5	13.5
SHARPE RATIO	0.49	0.73
MINIMUM RETURN (%)	-32.4	-17.3
MAXIMUM RETURN (%)	32.8	12.8
MAXIMUM DRAWDOWN (%)	-70.5	-46.7
SKEWNESS	-0.7	-1.0
KURTOSIS	10.7	5.9
PERCENT NEGATIVE PERIODS	39	31

The replicating portfolio dominates REITs in almost every way — it earns higher compound returns, has lower volatility, achieves a higher Sharpe ratio, has lower kurtosis and wins on most historical risk characteristics. A skeptic might note the replicating portfolio has a 33 percent allocation to long-term corporate bonds during a period in which interest rates have declined significantly, but the regression results show the term factor loading for the replicating portfolio is lower than the term factor loading for REITs. Thus, interest rate risk exposure cannot account for the results.

Kizer and Grover then tested REITs against their fourth criteria and concluded REITs fail to improve the mean-variance frontier, on a statistically inferred basis, when added to a portfolio holding established asset classes.

In summary, after first establishing a pragmatic list of criteria for considering asset classes, Kizer and Grover found that, while REITs do exhibit relatively low correlations with traditional equity and fixed income,

145

a deeper dive into REIT returns reveals a shortfall in its qualifications for recognition as a distinct asset class.

They found that multi-factor regression analyses revealed no statistically reliable alpha generation in REIT returns and that REIT returns are well explained by traditional risk factors. They also found that a long-only replication using small value equities and long-term corporate bonds produces a portfolio that co-moves well with REIT returns and exhibits historical risk and return characteristics generally better than REITs. Finally, they found that REITs do not reliably improve the mean-variance frontier when added to a benchmark portfolio of traditional stocks and bonds. These results, and the associated failure to satisfy their asset class criteria, led Kizer and Grover to conclude that REITs are not a distinct asset class.

FURTHER EVIDENCE

We now turn to a second study, "REITs in a Mixed-Asset Portfolio: An Investing of Extreme Risks," which appears in the Summer 2017 issue of *The Journal of Alternative Investments*. The authors, Steven Stelk, Jian Zhou and Randy Anderson, investigated the impact that adding REITs to a portfolio of stocks and bonds has had on value at risk (VaR) over the last two decades. VaR has become a standard measure of a portfolio's market risk, and it is used by both investors and regulators.

Perhaps Stelk, Zhou and Anderson were motivated by the fact that real estate was at the epicenter of the 2008 global financial crisis, and that REITs have become an increasingly popular investment vehicle. They note, for instance, that the market capitalization of U.S. REITs grew from $11.7 billion in 1989 to more than $907 billion in 2014. The authors may also have been motivated by the fact that, even though REITs had delivered higher returns than the S&P 500 Index, and did so with low correlation to both stocks and bonds, they recorded much higher volatility.

The following table shows annualized returns, standard deviations and Sharpe ratios for the Dow Jones U.S. Select REIT Index, the S&P 500 Index and five-year Treasury bonds over the period from January 1978 through May 2017.

	DOW JONES SELECT REIT INDEX	S&P 500 INDEX	FIVE-YEAR TREASURIES
ANNUALIZED RETURN (%)	12.2	11.7	7.1
ANNUAL STANDARD DEVIATION (%)	18.4	14.9	5.5
SHARPE RATIO	0.41	0.51	0.47

While the REIT index did provide higher returns, it did so with sufficiently greater volatility that the Sharpe ratio of the S&P 500 Index was 24 percent higher. The Sharpe ratio of five-year Treasury bonds was 15 percent higher. This is important in light of Kizer and Grover's finding that replicating portfolios were more mean-variant efficient than REITs.

Stelk, Zhou and Anderson began by reviewing some of the latest academic research on REITs. Among the research they cited was:

- Anderson, Vaneesha Boney and Hany Guirguis, authors of the 2012 study "The Impact of Switching Regimes and Monetary Shocks: An Empirical Analysis of REITs," found that unexpected monetary shocks affected REITs about twice as greatly as they affected the general equities market under high-variance regimes.

- A 2012 study from Zhou and Anderson, "Extreme Risk Measures for International REIT Markets," found that extreme risks for REITs generally were higher than those of the nine non-U.S. stock markets they studied, and that the timing of extreme market movements between REITs and stock indices was almost perfectly in sync. They concluded that the diversification benefits of REITs were sometimes not present when they were needed most.

- Kim Hiang Liow, who authored the 2008 study "Extreme Returns and Value at Risk in International Securitized Real Estate Markets," found REIT returns were riskier than the corresponding broader stock indices in each of the seven countries he considered.

- Jian Yang, Yinggang Zhou and Wai Kin Leung, authors of the 2012 study "Asymmetric Correlation and Volatility Dynamics among Stock, Bonds, and Securitized Real Estate Markets," found REIT returns exhibited stronger asymmetric correlations than stocks, bonds or even collateralized mortgage-backed securities over their sample period from 1999 through 2008. Asymmetric volatility was defined as increased return volatility after a negative shock.

- Martin Hoesli and Reka Kustrim, authors of the 2013 study "Volatility Spillovers, Comovements and Contagion in Securitized Real Estate Markets," analyzed the relationship between the volatility of securitized real estate markets and stock markets from 1990 to 2010, and found that equity returns were significantly more connected to the returns of securitized real estate when both markets were crashing compared to when they were booming.

- Luis Garcia-Feijoo, Gerald Jensen and Robert Johnson, authors of the 2012 study "The Effectiveness of Asset Classes in Hedging Risk," examined the diversification benefits of several categories of alternative investments on a mixed-asset portfolio. They found REIT returns had some of the highest correlations with stock and bond returns over their sample period of January 1970 through December 2010, and thus offered the lowest diversification benefits.

Based on the research they examined, Stelk, Zhou and Anderson concluded the "existing evidence suggests that REITs can provide portfolio diversification benefits under some market conditions, but not all. There is significant evidence that REITs may be harmful to a mixed-asset portfolio during times of market distress." Thus, the authors decided to explore what effects, if any, REITs have on the extreme risks of a mixed-asset portfolio.

Their data sample covered the U.S. REIT market during the period from 1989 through 2010. Their baseline portfolio held a traditional 60 percent stock/40 percent bond allocation. They then added a 10 percent and a 20 percent portfolio allocation to REITs, taking the REIT exposures equally from the stock and bond allocations. Finally, given the evidence that REITs have significant exposure to small-cap stock risk, they substituted small-cap stock exposure for the 10 percent and 20 percent REIT allocations. The following is a summary of the authors' findings:

- Adding REITs to a mixed-asset portfolio does not have a significant impact on the portfolio's average daily return or VaR before 2006 (prior to the first signs of the 2008 global financial crisis).

- After 2006, adding REITs to a portfolio of stocks and bonds significantly increases VaR. The increase in VaR is even greater than it is when adding small-cap stocks to the portfolio. The differences are significant at the 1 percent level.

- For a portfolio that already contains REITs (as a total-market fund would), adding additional weight to REITs further increases the portfolio's VaR.

Stelk, Zhou and Anderson concluded that the "increase in extreme downside risk during the financial crisis has significant risk management implications for REITs in a mixed-asset portfolio." They added: "Taken together, the results in this and previous studies do not dispute the long-run benefits of REITs, but they do raise questions about the role of REITs in a mixed-asset portfolio in times of financial crisis."

Before concluding, we have one additional study to examine.

THE CHANGING NATURE OF REITS

Stijn Van Nieuwerburgh, author of the April 2017 paper "Why Are REITs Currently So Expensive?", used common asset pricing models to show that there have been important changes in the nature of risk priced into REIT markets. We can see that for ourselves using the regression analysis tool available at Portfolio Visualizer (www.portfoliovisualizer.com), based on AQR data.

We will examine the results for Vanguard's REIT Index Investor Fund (VGSIX), the space's largest REIT fund with assets of more than $60 billion. From June 1996 through December 2007, the fund had the following loadings: market beta: 0.53; size: 0.38; value: 0.75; momentum: -0.05. The R-squared value of the model was 35 percent. However, from January 2008 through April 2017, the loadings shifted as follows: market beta: 1.02; size: 0.13; value: 0.46; momentum: -0.15. And the R-squared value rose to 59 percent (meaning the explanatory power of the model greatly increased). Clearly, compared to prior periods, stock risk became much more important while size and value risk became less important. Put another way, REITs moved more in conjunction with the market while becoming larger and more expensive. The result is that they lost factor diversification benefits.

Van Nieuwerburgh himself noted that "the stock beta of equity REITs peaks at 1.75 for the 5-year periods that end around 2009-10." In other words, consistent with preceding research, market risk for investors in REITs increased at exactly the wrong time. By the end of the period, the five-year market beta had fallen to 0.75, still well above historical levels.

Van Nieuwerburgh then looked at REITs' exposure to bond risk. He found that in addition to having larger exposure to market beta, REITs' interest-rate risk rose sharply over the last decade. The 10-year Treasury bond beta surged from zero before 2005 to 1.5 by December 2016. This indicates that, at a time when many investors are concerned about the potential for rising interest rates, REITs are now subject to significant interest-rate risk.

The twin findings of a dramatically higher market beta and the huge jump in 10-year Treasury bond beta mean that REIT investors are now subject to much greater risks than they historically experienced. Unfortunately, this comes at a time when both stock and bond (as well as REIT) valuations are at historically high levels — an inauspicious combination. It is one thing to have lots of risk and high risk premiums resulting from low valuations, which was the case in early 2009 when equity valuations were low. It is quite another to have high exposure to risk when valuations are high, and expected returns are therefore lower.

SUMMARY

Neither Kizer and Grover, nor Stelk, Zhou and Anderson, recommend excluding REITs from equity portfolios. Instead, their results should lead investors to conclude that REITs are an equity security with only marginal diversification benefits. Thus, they should not receive a weighting in investor portfolios greater than market-capitalization-based weights. According to data from Morningstar, REITs currently represent approximately 3.7 percent of the iShares Russell 3000 ETF (IWV) on a market-capitalization basis, which is a valid starting point for a REIT allocation in a diversified portfolio.

This is the approach we take at my firm, Buckingham Strategic Wealth. Because the equity mutual funds we utilize exclude REITs in their design, the allocation (typically about 3 percent) to REITs is accomplished through a separate allocation to a passively managed REIT fund, such as VGSIX. With that said, given the evidence, and the increase in correlations to both stocks and bonds, investors more concerned about downside risk should consider a reduced allocation to this asset class. This is especially true for investors with limited space in their tax-advantaged accounts, in which case REITs might crowd out investments with superior diversification benefits.

In closing, investors need to recognize that, over the long term, real growth in REIT dividends has been about -0.7 percent. While no one knows what the future holds for REIT returns, at the very least, REIT investors should be aware of the nature of these changes and their implications. Thus, when forecasting future real expected returns to REITs, you should subtract 0.7 percentage points from the current yield.

APPENDIX D: HOW TO EVALUATE INDEX AND PASSIVE FUNDS

For evidence-based investors, selecting an investment vehicle is much simpler than it is for active investors because the universe of funds from which to choose is much smaller. However, even for evidence-based investors, the decision is not as simple as looking at the expense ratios of the various options within each asset class and choosing the cheapest fund. The reason is that not all "index" funds are created equal.

While expense ratio is an important consideration, it should not be the only one. In practice, a more expensive fund manager can add value in several ways that have nothing to do with "active" investing. (Active investing is defined as the use of either technical or fundamental analysis to identify specific securities to either overweight or underweight). Let's explore some of the ways a fund can add value in terms of portfolio construction, tax management and/or trading strategies.

1. CHOICE OF BENCHMARK INDEX OR HOW A FUND DEFINES ITS INVESTMENT UNIVERSE

This decision affects returns in several important ways:

- Turnover, which impacts trading costs and tax efficiency. Some indices have higher turnover than others. And some indices/funds have added hold ranges (the index/fund will no longer buy additional shares, but it will not sell existing holdings) designed to reduce the negative impact of turnover (both on transaction costs and tax efficiency).

- Exposure to the size and value risk factors. The greater the exposure, the higher the risk and expected return of the fund.

As an example, let us look at two such funds: the DFA U.S. Small Cap Value Portfolio (DFSVX) and the Vanguard Small-Cap Value Index Fund (VISVX). The table shows their expense ratios and degree of exposure to the market beta, size and value premiums for the period from June 1998 (VISVX's inception date) through December 2016. The data comes from the regression tool available at Portfolio Visualizer (www.portfoliovisualizer.com).

	MARKET PREMIUM EXPOSURE	SIZE PREMIUM EXPOSURE	VALUE PREMIUM EXPOSURE	EXPENSE RATIO
DFSVX	1.02	0.79	0.65	0.52%
VISVX*	1.00	0.52	0.61	0.19%

*Vanguard now has an admiral shares version of its small-cap value index fund with an expense ratio of just 0.07 percent.

The point is not to say that one fund is necessarily better than the other. The lesson is that not all passive funds are created equal, and you should not simply look at expense ratios and end your evaluation there. Instead, determine how much exposure you need to the market beta, size and value premiums, and then find the least expensive way of getting that exposure. Remember, the more exposure you have to the size and value premiums, the less equity risk you need to hold to achieve the same expected return.

Now, resuming our list of ways that a fund's benchmark index or investment universe can affect returns:

- Correlation of the fund to other portfolio assets (the lower the correlation, the more effective the diversification).

- Some indices are more opaque than others, preventing actively managed funds from exploiting the "forced turnover" created when indices reconstitute (typically annually). A lack of opaqueness historically has created problems for index funds that replicate the Russell 2000 Index.

- A fund can add value through incorporating the momentum effect by temporarily delaying the purchase of stocks exhibiting negative momentum and by temporarily delaying the sale of stocks exhibiting positive momentum. It can also add value by incorporating the profitability factor.

- A fund can screen out certain securities (even if they are within the defined index) with characteristics that have demonstrated poor risk/return profiles (such as stocks in bankruptcy, very low-priced stocks, IPOs and extreme small growth stocks). For example, while utilities and real estate stocks typically have high book-to-market ratios (and, therefore, are found in most value indices) they also have very low market betas (exposure to equity risk). Including them in value indices that use book-to-market ratio as the screen creates a drag on returns. In addition, including real estate in value funds will make the fund less tax efficient (because the dividends from REITs are non-qualified and thus taxed as ordinary income).

- How often an index reconstitutes can impact returns. Most indices (such as the Russell and RAFI Fundamental Indices) reconstitute annually. A lack of frequent reconstitution can create significant style drift. For example, from 1990 through 2006, the percentage of stocks in the Russell 2000 in June that would leave the index when it reconstituted at the end of the month was 20 percent. For the Russell 2000 Value Index, the figure was 28 percent. Over the course of the year, a small-cap index fund based on the Russell 2000 would have seen its exposure to the size factor drift lower. For small value funds based on the Russell 2000 Value Index, exposure to both the size and value premiums would have drifted lower. Drift toward lower factor exposure results in lower expected returns, as well as less factor diversification.

2. PATIENT TRADING

If a fund's goal is to replicate an index, it must trade when stocks enter or exit that index. It must also hold the exact weighting of each security in the index. A fund whose goal is to earn the return of the asset class, and that is willing to live with some random tracking error relative to its benchmark index, can be more patient in its trading strategy, using market orders and block trading to take advantage of discounts offered by active managers looking to quickly sell large blocks of stock. Patient trading reduces transaction costs and block trading can even create negative trading costs in some cases.

3. TAX MANAGEMENT

While indexing is a relatively tax efficient strategy (due to relatively low turnover), strategies can be employed that improve tax efficiency:

- Harvest losses whenever they are significant.

- Eliminate any unintentional short-term capital gains (those not the result of acquisitions).

- Create wider buy and hold ranges to reduce turnover.

- Preserve qualified dividends, which are taxed at lower rates. A fund must own stock that earns dividends for more than 60 days of a prescribed 121-day period. That period begins 60 days prior to the ex-dividend date.

- Limit securities lending revenue to the expense ratio.

4. MULTIPLE VALUE SCREENS

Academic research on stock returns has documented that value stocks historically have outperformed growth stocks. We see the higher returns to value stocks in almost all countries. Not only has value outperformed growth, but the persistence of its outperformance has been greater than the persistence of stocks outperforming bonds.

Many different metrics can be used in implementing a value strategy. Among the most common are price-to-earnings ratio, price-to-sales ratio, price-to-book value ratio, price-to-dividends ratio and price-to-cash flow ratio. The various metrics all produce results showing that value stocks have had higher returns than growth stocks. And the various measures produce similar results (with the weakest results coming from the price-to-dividend ratio).

Given the similarity in results, price-to-book ratio has been the most widely used because book value is more stable over time than the other metrics. That helps keep portfolio turnover down, which in turn helps keeps trading costs down and tax efficiency higher. Recently, some passively managed funds have moved away from a single-screen metric because research indicates that using multiple screens produces better results. Part of the reasoning is that price-to-book ratio can work well as a value metric in some industries/sectors, but not in others. With this in mind, it could make sense to use multiple value metrics instead of sorting exclusively by price-to-book. Another reason is that different value metrics (such as price-to-earnings, price-to-cash flow and price-to-EBITDA), while highly correlated, are not perfectly correlated. Thus, the use of multiple value metrics provides a diversification benefit. A third benefit of multiple metrics is that value measures such as price-to-cash flow offer more exposure to the profitability and quality factors, increasing factor diversification and helping to avoid "value traps" (stocks that may look cheap on a price-to-book ratio basis, but could be overvalued).

5. SECURITIES LENDING

Securities lending refers to the lending of securities by one party to another. Securities are often borrowed with the intent to sell them short. In the international markets, another reason for securities lending has to do with exploiting the foreign tax credit. Thus, the opportunities to add value are greater in foreign markets. As payment for the loan of the security, parties negotiate a fee. Some mutual funds are more aggressive than others in this area.

The following example demonstrates why it is a mistake to only look at a fund's operating expense ratio. Let us assume that Fund A has an expense ratio of 55 basis points and generates 40 basis points in securities lending fees that are credited to the fund (not the fund manager). Thus, we might consider the fund's "net" expenses to be 15 basis points. Fund B in the same asset class has a significantly lower expense ratio at 35 basis points. However, it generates just 12 basis points in securities lending fees. Thus, its "net" expenses of 23 basis points exceed Fund A's "net" expenses of 15 basis points. Securities lending revenue data is available in the mutual funds' annual reports.

6. CORE FUNDS

Core funds combine multiple asset classes into a single fund. Fund managers developed the core approach because it is the most efficient way to hold multiple asset classes, especially for taxable accounts. The following example will demonstrate why this is the case.

The Russell 3000 can be broken down into four components: the stocks that make up the Russell 1000 Growth Index, the stocks that make up the Russell 1000 Value Index, the stocks that make up the Russell 2000 Growth Index and the stocks that make up the Russell 2000 Value Index. We have seen institutions hold all four components in exactly the same market-cap weighting that the Russell 3000 holds them. In other words, they owned the same stocks, in the very same proportions, as the Russell 3000 — only in four funds instead of one. This makes no sense because when the indices reconstitute each June, each of the four component index funds will have to sell the stocks that leave its index and buy the stocks that enter its index. That incurs transaction costs, which can be particularly large when the entire market knows you have to trade, and especially large for small-cap stocks. In addition, if a stock moves asset classes from value to growth or vice versa, this could mean that one component index fund you own sells the stock only to have another component index fund you own buy it. The benefits of owning the single fund are obvious.

Now consider an investor who owns four component U.S. index funds, a large company fund, a small company fund, a large value fund and a small value fund. A single fund that held the same stocks, in the same proportions, would be a more efficient approach. Dimensional Fund Advisors (DFA) has created core funds with various degrees of "tilt" (meaning they depart from market-cap weightings) to small-cap and value stocks. The benefits are reduced turnover — which reduces transaction costs and the realization of capital gains — and the minimization of the need for investors to rebalance. (The fund itself rebalances using dividends and cash flows.) Each of these can provide significant benefits, especially for taxable accounts.

Another example of a core fund is the Vanguard Total International Stock Index Fund (VGTSX), which combines holdings in developed and emerging markets. This is a significant improvement for investors who previously would have had to hold the two components separately. A single fund will avoid having to sell and buy stocks from a country that migrates from an emerging to a developed market, as Israel did recently and South Korea and Taiwan are expected to do. This not only minimizes transaction costs in markets where they can be quite high, but it also avoids, or at least minimizes, the realization of capital gains. It also eliminates the need for investors to rebalance the portfolio, yet again helping them to avoid trading costs and the realization of capital gains. The fund itself rebalances with "other people's money," using cash flows and dividends.

Core funds are just another example of how financial engineering can add value through structuring portfolios, without trying to add value (with low odds of success) by generating alpha from stock-picking or market-timing strategies.

SUMMARY

As author John Ruskin explained: "Not only is there but one way of doing things rightly, but there is only one way of seeing them, and that is, seeing the whole of them." While certain funds may be the cheapest in terms of expense ratios, when evaluating similar passively managed mutual funds, it is important to consider not only the operating expense ratio, but also all the ways a fund can add value. A little bit of extra homework can pay significant dividends.

APPENDIX E: ENOUGH

To know you have enough is to be rich.
—The Tao Te Ching

Author Kurt Vonnegut related this story about fellow author Joseph Heller: "Heller and I were at a party given by a billionaire on Shelter Island. I said, 'Joe, how does it make you feel to know that our host only yesterday may have made more money than your novel *Catch-22* has earned in its entire history?' Joe said, 'I've got something he can never have.' And I said, 'What on earth could that be, Joe?' And Joe said, 'The knowledge that I've got *enough*.'"

What Heller was saying was that you are rich when you know you have enough. Of course, everyone's definition of "enough" is different. From the perspective of an investment plan, how you define enough is of great importance because it defines your need to take risk — the rate of return you require to achieve your financial goals. The more you convert *desires* (what might be called "nice-to-haves") into *needs* ("must-haves"), the larger the portfolio you will need to support that lifestyle. And the more risk you will need to take to achieve that goal.

Those with sufficient wealth to meet all their needs should consider that the strategy to get rich is entirely different from the strategy to stay rich. The strategy to get rich is to take risks, and concentrate them, typically in one's own business. However, the strategy to stay rich is to minimize risk, diversify the risks you do take, and to avoid spending too much. In other words, if you have already won the game — meaning you have a large enough portfolio to meet all your needs — it is time to change your strategy and develop a new investment plan. The new plan should be based on the fact that the inconvenience of going from having enough to not having enough is unthinkable.

When deciding on the appropriate asset allocation, investors should consider their *marginal utility of wealth* — how much any potential incremental gain in wealth is worth relative to the risk that must be accepted to achieve a greater *expected* return. While more money is always better than less, at some point many people achieve a lifestyle with which they are very comfortable. At that point, taking on incremental risk to achieve a higher net worth no longer makes sense: The potential damage of an unexpected negative outcome far exceeds the potential benefit gained from incremental wealth. The utility curve in the following chart illustrates this point.

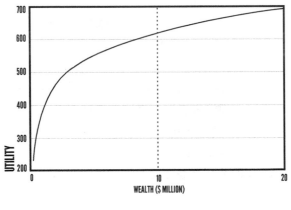

Each investor needs to decide at what level of wealth their unique utility of wealth curve starts flattening out and bending sharply to the right. In the preceding example, that point is about $10 million. For you, it might be $500,000 or $1 million. There is no one right answer. Just an answer that is right for each individual. However, whether the figure is $1 million or $50 million, beyond this point there is little reason to take incremental risk to achieve a higher expected return. Many wealthy investors have experienced devastating losses (does the name Madoff ring a bell?) that could easily have been avoided if they had the wisdom to know what author Joseph Heller understood.

A lesson about knowing when enough is enough can be gleaned from the following incident. In early 2003, Larry met with a 71-year-old couple with financial assets of $3 million. Three years earlier, their portfolio had been worth $13 million. The only way they could have experienced that kind of loss was if they had held a portfolio almost all in equities and heavily concentrated in U.S. large-cap growth stocks, especially technology stocks. They confirmed this. They then told him they had been working with a financial advisor during this period — demonstrating that while good advice does not have to be expensive, bad advice almost always costs you dearly.

Larry asked the couple whether any meaningful change in the quality of their lives would have occurred if, instead of their portfolio having fallen almost 80 percent, it had doubled to $26 million. The response was a definitive no. Larry then noted that the experience of watching $13 million shrink to $3 million must have been very painful, and that they probably had spent many sleepless nights. They agreed. He then asked why they had taken the risks they did, knowing the potential benefit was not going to change their lives very much, but a negative outcome like the one they experienced would be so painful.

The wife turned to the husband and punched him, exclaiming, "I told you so!"

Some risks are not worth taking. Prudent investors do not assume more risk than they have the ability, willingness or *need* to take. The important question to ask yourself is: If you've already won the game, why are you still playing?

NEEDS VS. DESIRES

One reason people continue to play a game they have already won is that they convert what were once desires (things nice to have, but not necessary to enjoy life) into needs. That calculus increases the need to take risk. That, in turn, causes an increase in the required equity allocation. And, that can lead to problems when risks show up, as they did in 1973-1974, 2000-2002 and again in 2007-2008.

MORAL OF THE TALE

Failing to consider the need to take risk is a mistake common to many wealthy people, especially those who became wealthy by taking large risks. However, the mistake of taking more risk than necessary is not limited to the very wealthy. Ask yourself how much money buys happiness. Most people would be surprised to find that the figure they come up with is a lot less than they thought. For example, psychologists have found that once you have enough money to meet basic needs like food, shelter and health care, incremental increases have little effect on your happiness. Once you have met those requirements, the good things in life (the really important things) are either free or cheap. For instance, taking a walk in a park with your significant other, riding a bike, reading a book, playing bridge with friends or playing with your children/grandchildren does not cost very much if anything. And switching from a $20 bottle of wine to a $100 bottle of wine, or from eating in a restaurant that costs $50 for dinner for two to one that costs $500, likely won't really make you any happier. Moreover, even a $50 dinner every evening likely does not yield a whole lot more happiness than a $50 dinner every other evening.

When developing your investment policy statement, make sure you have differentiated between needs and desires, and then carefully consider your marginal utility of incremental wealth so you can determine if those desires are worth the incremental risks that you will have to accept. Knowing when you have enough is one of the keys to playing the winner's game in both life and investing.

APPENDIX F: IMPLEMENTATION [MUTUAL FUNDS AND ETFs]

The following list of funds has been approved by the investment policy committee at Buckingham Strategic Wealth.[1] Thus, these are the products we believe you should consider first when constructing your portfolio. Where more than one share class for a mutual fund is available, the lowest-cost version is shown. That fund version may not be available to all investors because minimums may be required. AQR, Bridgeway and DFA funds are available through approved financial advisors and in retirement and 529 plans. (Note that for some AQR funds, lower-cost R Share versions may be available to some investors.) Considerations for selecting a fund should include how much exposure it provides to each desired/targeted factor, its expense ratio, and the

---

[1] Provided for informational purposes only and is not intended to serve as specific investment or financial advice. This list of funds does not constitute a recommendation to purchase a single specific security and it should not be assumed that the securities referenced herein were or will prove to be profitable. Prior to making any investment, an investor should carefully consider the fund's risks and investment objectives and evaluate all offering materials and other documents associated with the investment.

amount of diversification it offers (that is, the number of securities held and their weightings). For ETFs, the liquidity of the fund is an added consideration. Our recommendation is that the ETFs you consider have more than $100 million in assets and an average daily trading volume in excess of $5 million.

SINGLE-STYLE FUNDS

MARKET BETA

DOMESTIC

FIDELITY SPARTAN TOTAL MARKET INDEX (FSTVX)
SCHWAB U.S. BROAD MARKET (SCHB)
VANGUARD TOTAL STOCK MARKET INDEX (VTI/VTSAX)
ISHARES CORE S&P TOTAL US MARKET (ITOT)

INTERNATIONAL DEVELOPED MARKETS

FIDELITY SPARTAN INTERNATIONAL INDEX (FSIIX)
VANGUARD FTSE ALL-WORLD EX-US (VEU/VFWAX)
VANGUARD TOTAL INTERNATIONAL STOCK (VXUS/VTIAX)
SCHWAB INTERNATIONAL EQUITY (SCHF)
ISHARES CORE MSCI EAFE (IEFA)

EMERGING MARKETS

DFA EMERGING MARKETS (DFEMX)
SCHWAB EMERGING MARKETS (SCHE)
VANGUARD FTSE EMERGING MARKETS (VWO/VEMAX)

SMALL

DOMESTIC

BRIDGEWAY ULTRA-SMALL COMPANY MARKET (BRSIX)
DFA US MICRO CAP (DFSCX)
DFA US SMALL CAP (DFSTX)
ISHARES RUSSELL MICROCAP (IWC)
VANGUARD SMALL CAP INDEX FUND (VB/VSMAX)
SCHWAB U.S. SMALL CAP (SCHA)
ISHARES CORE S&P SMALL-CAP (IJR)

INTERNATIONAL DEVELOPED MARKETS

DFA INTERNATIONAL SMALL COMPANY (DFISX)
SPDR S&P INTERNATIONAL SMALL CAP ETF (GWX)
VANGUARD FTSE ALL-WORLD EX-US SMALLCAP (VSS/VFSVX)
SCHWAB INTERNATIONAL SMALL-CAP EQUITY (SCHC)

EMERGING MARKETS

DFA EMERGING MARKETS SMALL (DEMSX)
SPDR S&P EMERGING MARKETS SMALL CAP (EWX)

LARGE AND VALUE

DOMESTIC

DFA US LARGE CAP VALUE III (DFUVX)
DFA TAX-MANAGED US MARKETWIDE VALUE II (DFMVX)
SCHWAB US LARGE-CAP VALUE (SCHV)
VANGUARD VALUE INDEX (VTV/VVIAX)

INTERNATIONAL DEVELOPED MARKETS

DFA INTERNATIONAL VALUE III (DFVIX)
DFA TAX-MANAGED INTERNATIONAL VALUE (DTMIX)
ISHARES MSCI EAFE VALUE (EFV)

EMERGING MARKETS

DFA EMERGING MARKETS VALUE (DFEVX)

SMALL AND VALUE

DOMESTIC

BRIDGEWAY OMNI SMALL CAP VALUE (BOSVX)
BRIDGEWAY OMNI TAX-MANAGED SMALL-CAP VALUE (BOTSX)
DFA US SMALL CAP VALUE (DFSVX)
DFA TAX-MANAGED US TARGETED VALUE (DTMVX)
ISHARES S&P SMALL-CAP 600 VALUE (IJS)
SPDR S&P 600 SMALL CAP VALUE ETF (SLYV)
VANGUARD SMALL CAP VALUE (VBR/VSIAX)

INTERNATIONAL DEVELOPED MARKETS

DFA INT'L SMALL CAP VALUE (DISVX)
DFA WORLD EX US TARGETED VALUE (DWUSX)

MOMENTUM

DOMESTIC

AQR MOMENTUM (AMOMX)
ISHARES MSCI USA MOMENTUM FACTOR (MTUM)

INTERNATIONAL DEVELOPED MARKETS

AQR INTERNATIONAL MOMENTUM (AIMOX)

PROFITABILITY/QUALITY

DOMESTIC

ISHARES MSCI USA QUALITY FACTOR ETF (QUAL)

INTERNATIONAL DEVELOPED MARKETS

ISHARES MSCI INTERNATIONAL DEVELOPED QUALITY FACTOR ETF (IQLT)

TERM

DFA FIVE-YEAR GLOBAL FIXED INCOME (DFGBX)
ISHARES BARCLAYS 7-10 YEAR TREASURY (IEF)
ISHARES US TREASURY BOND ETF (GOVT)
VANGUARD INTERMEDIATE-TERM TREASURY (VGIT/VFIUX)

CARRY

POWERSHARES DB G10 CURRENCY HARVEST ETF (DBV)

MULTI-STYLE FUNDS

SMALL + VALUE + PROFITABILITY/QUALITY

DOMESTIC

DFA US CORE EQUITY 2 (DFQTX)
DFA TA US CORE EQUITY 2 (DFTCX)

INTERNATIONAL

DFA INT'L CORE EQUITY (DFIEX)
DFA TA WORLD EX US CORE EQUITY (DFTWX)

VALUE + MOMENTUM + PROFITABILITY/QUALITY

DOMESTIC

AQR LARGE CAP MULTI-STYLE (QCELX)
ISHARES EDGE MSCI MULTIFACTOR USA ETF (LRGF)

INTERNATIONAL

AQR INTERNATIONAL MULTI-STYLE (QICLX)

SMALL + VALUE + MOMENTUM
+ PROFITABILITY/QUALITY

AQR SMALL CAP MULTI-STYLE (QSMLX)

VALUE + MOMENTUM + QUALITY + DEFENSIVE
(STOCKS, BONDS, CURRENCIES AND COMMODITIES)

AQR STYLE PREMIA (QSPIX)

TREND-FOLLOWING
(STOCKS, BONDS, CURRENCIES AND COMMODITIES)

AQR MANAGED FUTURES (AQMIX)

ALTERNATIVE FUNDS

ALTERNATIVE LENDING

STONE RIDGE ALTERNATIVE LENDING RISK PREMIUM INTERVAL FUND (LENDX)

REINSURANCE

STONE RIDGE REINSURANCE RISK PREMIUM INTERVAL FUND (SRRIX)

VARIANCE RISK PREMIUM

STONE RIDGE ALL ASSET VARIANCE RISK PREMIUM INTERVAL FUND (AVRPX)

SOURCES OF DATA

S&P Dow Jones Indices for data on the S&P 500 Index and the S&P GSCI. Used with permission.

Kenneth R. French, the Center for Research in Security Prices (CRSP) at the University of Chicago and Fama/French Data Library for data on the various Fama-French series. Used with permission.

Morgan Stanley for data on the MSCI indices (www.msci.com). Used with permission. The MSCI data contained herein is the property of MSCI Inc. (MSCI). MSCI, its affiliates and its information providers make no warranties with respect to any such data. The MSCI data contained herein is used under license and may not be further used, distributed or disseminated without the express written consent of MSCI.

Morningstar for data on five-year Treasury notes. Used with permission. © 2017 Morningstar, Inc. All rights reserved. The information contained herein: (1) is proprietary to Morningstar and/or its content providers; (2) may not be copied or distributed; (3) does not constitute investment advice offered by Morningstar; and (4) is not warranted to be accurate, complete or timely. Neither Morningstar nor its content providers are responsible for any damages or losses arising from any use of this information. Past performance is no guarantee of future results. Use of information from Morningstar does not necessarily constitute agreement by Morningstar, Inc. of any investment philosophy or strategy presented in this publication.